The essence of my life is this:
A baby's smile, a loved one's kiss
A book, a song, the sea, a friend
And just a little time to spend

Seeds of Greatness

sound wisdom
Because Your Success Matters

Published and distributed by:
SOUND WISDOM
P.O. Box 310
Shippensburg, PA 17257-0310
717-530-2122

info@soundwisdom.com

www.soundwisdom.com

ISBN 13 TP: 978-1-64095-569-1

ISBN 13 eBook: 978-1-64095-570-7

For Worldwide Distribution, Printed in the U.S.A.

1 2 3 4 5 6 7 8 / 29 28 27 26 25

A Priceless Gift of
Poetry, Prose, & Proverbs
of Inspiration

Seeds of Greatness

TREASURY

From the best-selling author of
The Psychology of Winning & Being the Best

DENIS WAITLEY

Contents

Prologue

The Seeds of Greatness

My grandma, Mabel Reynolds Ostrander, and I shared one of those special relationships as rare as a double rainbow. She was fifty-three when I was ten. That's when we planted our first "Victory" garden together during World War II. We planted seeds together—in the soil—and in each other.

Grandma lived eighty-seven seasons without a complaint. I was forty-four when I last saw her. But I remember every mince and lemon tart, every bite of made-from-scratch apple pie, and every lingering wave of her hand as she stood (out of sight or so she thought) behind the rayon Priscilla curtains in the little house at 718 West Pennsylvania Avenue in San Diego, California, where I was born and raised. Later in life, as our station wagon full of my kids, and contentment, would slowly pull away from the curb, we would all look back at her and wave—and I would gaze at her fragile silhouette through the rear-view mirror, wishing I could frame her there forever, just that way—wondering how many more Easter and Christmas dinners we would share.

Most of all, I remember my grandma and me planting seeds. We planted squash, beans, corn, watermelons, beets, pansies, mums, and other flowers. I'll admit I rode my bike those twenty miles each Saturday more for the bonus of the conversation and the homemade pastries, than for the vegetables and flowers. But no matter how full I was after I ate, I was always left hungry for more of the wisdom and optimism she shared with me.

I'll never forget the day we tasted our first harvest as a result of crossing a plum tree with an apricot tree. The ripe fruit was pink, not purple like a plum, nor orange like an apricot; but a combination of both. "Gee, do you suppose they'll be any good?" I asked. "Why, of course, they will be wonderful," she chided. "Didn't we do the planting, nurturing, and pruning?"

Sure enough, they were delicious, even though they were different than any fruit I'd ever seen before. "That's because they are uniquely unlike any other fruit you'll ever eat. They are plumcots!" she exulted. "You always get out what you put in," she continued as we sat under the tree eating most of what we had picked.

"Plant apple seeds and you get apple trees, plant acorns and you get majestic oak trees, plant weeds and you will harvest weeds (even without watering), plant the seeds of great ideas and you will get great individuals," she said softly and intently, looking directly into my eyes. "Do you understand what I mean?" I nodded, remembering I'd heard her say the same thing before, in different ways.

I learned from my grandma that the seeds of greatness are not special genes dependent on the birth of the gifted, the inherited bank account, the intellect, the skin-deep beauty, the race, the gender, or the status. The seeds of greatness are attitudes and beliefs that begin in children by observing, imitating, and internalizing the lifestyles of significant role models and heroes.

"Model your thoughts and actions after men and women who have been passionate, excellent, honest, unselfish, and creative in their service to others," my grandmother counseled. Armed with that affirmation, I ventured forth to sow and reap my own legacy in life. ❧

I've traveled the world to the seven seas.
I've been up at the top and down on my knees.
I've been blessed with abundance and plenty of weeds.
But I've never stopped caring about others' needs.

As you tend your own garden, unlike any other.
Remember the words of my lovely grandmother.
"If you're hoping to harvest a life of great deeds,
remember you first have to plant some great seeds."

Chapter One

Seeds of Determination

IT'S UP TO ME

As We Sow, So Shall We Harvest

Our true rewards in life will depend on the quality and amount of contribution we make. From the Scriptures, to science, to psychology, to business, the documentation is the same. "As we sow, we reap." Life is an unfailing boomerang. What we throw out will come back full circle.

The way we can build self-reliance is to recognize the number of alternative choices we have in a free society. And for every choice we make, there is a consequence or reward of that decision that we must acknowledge as our responsibility. God's law of cause and effect is forever the ruler.

During debriefing interviews, returning POWs from the wars in which we have fought during the past century said that what they missed most of all was their freedom of choice. There are two primary choices in our lives: to accept conditions as they exist or to accept the responsibility for changing them.

To attain emotional security, each of us must learn to develop two critical capabilities: the ability to live with uncertainty, and the ability to delay immediate gratification in favor of long-range goals. Losers let life happen to them. Winners make it happen for themselves and others. Losers engage in pleasurable activities, with no purpose or result in mind. Losers try to escape from their fears and drudgery with activities that are tension relieving. Winners are motivated by their desires toward activities that are goal achieving.

A number of research studies during the past decade indicate that the happiest, most well-adjusted individuals are those who believe they have a strong measure of control over their lives. They choose more appropriate responses to what occurs and they stand up to inevitable changes and daily setbacks with less apprehension. They learn from their past mistakes, rather than reinforce or repeat them. They spend time taking action in the present, rather than fearing what might happen in the future.

To be self-reliant adults, we need some guidelines:

- Be different if it means higher personal and professional standards.

- Be different if it means being more gracious and considerate to others.

- Be different if it means being cleaner, neater, and better groomed than the group.

- Be different if it means putting more time and effort into all you do.

- And be different if it means taking the calculated risk. The greatest risk in life is to wait for and depend upon others for your own security. The greatest security is to plan and act, and take the risk that will ultimately ensure your personal freedom and independence.

It's not what happens to you in
life that counts, it's how you take
it and what you make of it.

The only person who never
makes mistakes is the person
who never does anything.

If there is no wind, row!

The few who do are the envy of
the many who only watch.

Indecision is the thief of opportunity.

The self-help books you
don't read won't help!

Life is a do-it-for-others,
do-it-yourself project.

The greatest risk is to do nothing.

Those who seek security are
no longer employable.

Stop stewing and start doing!
Take action TNT.
Today, Not Tomorrow.

Someday I'll

There is an island fantasy
A "Someday I'll," we'll never see
Where stocks stay up and hunger ceases
Our jobs are secure and our pay increases

That "Someday I'll," where problems end
Where every call and e-mail is from a friend
Where the children are sweet, already grown
Where all the other nations can go it alone
Where we all retire at forty-one
Playing backgammon in the tropical sun

Most unhappy people look to tomorrow
To erase this day's hardship and sorrow
They put happiness on layaway
And struggle through a blue today

But happiness cannot be sought
It can't be owned, it can't be bought
Life's most important revelation
The journey means more than the destination

Happiness is where you are right now
Pushing a pencil or pushing a plow
It's going to school or standing in line
Watching and waiting, or tasting the wine
If you live in the past you become senile
If you live in the future you're on "Someday I'll"

The fear of results is procrastination
The joy of today is a celebration
You can save, you can slave, trudging mile after mile
But you'll never set foot on your "Someday I'll"

When you've paid all your dues and put in your time
Out of nowhere comes another Mt. Everest to climb
From this day forward make it your vow
Take "Someday I'll" and make it your Now!

Making the Most of Today

What each of us is doing this minute is the most important event in history for us. We have decided to invest our resources in this opportunity more than any other.

As the years pass, I am acutely aware that the bird of time is on the wing. At my fortieth high school reunion, I saw old people who claimed to be my former classmates. We all had big name tags printed in capital letters so we wouldn't have to squint with our reading glasses trying to associate the name with each well-traveled face. It seemed like only yesterday that I was enjoying high school. What had happened to the decades in between? Where had they flown?

To the side of the bandstand where the big-band sound of the 1950s blared our favorite top-ten hits, there was a poster with a printed verse for all of us to see. I went to the microphone and read the words aloud for my friends:

"There are two days in every week about which we should not worry, two days which should be kept free from fear and apprehension.

One of these days is **Yesterday**, with its mistakes and cares, its faults and blunders, its aches and pains. Yesterday has passed forever beyond our control. All the money in the world cannot bring back Yesterday. We cannot undo a single act we performed; we cannot erase a single word we said. Yesterday is gone.

The other day we should not worry about is **Tomorrow**, with its possible adversities, its burdens, its large promise, and poor performance. Tomorrow is also beyond our immediate control.

Tomorrow's sun will rise, either in splendor or behind a mask of clouds, but it will rise. Until it does, we have no stake in tomorrow, for it is as yet unborn.

This leaves only one day: **Today**. Anyone can fight the battles of just one day. It is only when you and I add the burdens of those two awful eternities—Yesterday and Tomorrow—that we break down.

It is not the experience of Today that drives us mad, it is remorse and bitterness for something which happened Yesterday and the dread of what Tomorrow may bring.

Let us therefore, live this one full Today."[1] ❧

---

1. Waitley, Denis, *The Psychology of Motivation* (Chicago, Illinois: Nightingale-Conant Corp., 1997) pp 331-332.

Procrastination is a favorite hiding place.

Depending on the government for your future financial security is like hiring an accountant who is a compulsive gambler!

Life is not accountable to us for meaning, we are accountable to life.

Everything that is past is either a learning experience to grow from, a beautiful memory to reflect on, or a motivating factor to act upon.

By thinking and acting affirmatively in this minute, you will influence the hour, the day, and in time, your entire life.

Our rewards in life will depend on the quality and amount of contribution we make.

I would rather fail in trying, than succeed in doing nothing.

If you concentrate on the present,
you eliminate what happened
yesterday and any apprehension
of what may happen tomorrow.

The greatest risk in life is to wait for and
depend upon others for your security.
The greatest security is to plan and take
the risk that will make you independent.

You have been given the greatest power
in the world—the power to choose.

Maintaining the Status Quo

When I was doing research for *The Psychology of Winning*, my first major work, I came across a study of a South American tribe whose members had been dying prematurely for generations. The cause was a rare disease. Scientists finally discovered it was carried by an insect that lived in the walls of their adobe lodgings. The natives had a choice of several solutions. They could destroy the insects with a pesticide. They could tear down and rebuild their houses. They could move to where that species of insects didn't live. Or they could do nothing and continue to die young.

In the end, they chose the last alternative. And although that might sound incredible to us, I meet many people with a similar attitude toward achieving personal success. Knowing that certain changes would make that much more likely for them, they nevertheless take the path of least resistance, no change. For the temporary, often illusory comfort of staying as they are, they pay the terrible price of a life not truly lived. 🦌

There was a very cautious man
Who never laughed or cried.
He never risked, he never lost,
he never won nor tried.

And when he one day passed away
His insurance was denied,
For since he never really lived,
They claimed he never died!

Chapter Two

Seeds of Belief

ATTITUDE IS EVERYTHING

The Power of Faith

When we talk about faith—and belief—we have to turn to the Scriptures. "Go thy way, and as thou hast believed, so be it done unto thee."

This simple statement cuts both ways, like a two-edged sword. Faith is the key to unlock the door of success for every human being. Or it is the lock that imprisons and prevents that human being from ever experiencing success.

Here is a power which every person has, but which few people use consciously. One individual does not possess this power above another, or to a greater degree. Everyone has it, since everyone lives and has consciousness. The question then is not: "Do we have this power? It is merely, are we using it correctly?"

As a positive power, faith is the promise of the realization of things hoped for and unforeseen. As a negative power, it is the premonition of our deepest fears and unseen darkness. There is no such thing as the absence of or lack of faith. There is simply the replacement of faith, with its opposite belief—despair.

Much has been written through the ages and discussed concerning the *self-fulfilling prophecy*. The self-fulfilling prophecy is a statement that is not necessarily true or false, but is capable of becoming true for us as individuals or groups if it is believed.

Science and religion are very closely allied in the implications resulting from studies of the brain during recent years. Although we have much to learn in understanding the chemistry and mechanisms in the brain and central nervous system, we are aware of the inextricable relationship between psyche and soma—mind and body. There is a definite reaction in the body as the result of the thoughts and concerns of the mind.

This is why the concepts of faith and belief are so important. What the mind harbors, the body manifests in some way. ❧

Your attitude is either the lock on
or key to your door of success.

One person's ceiling is
another person's floor.

It's not what you are that holds you
back, it's what you think you're not.

Better to seek change by inspiration
than out of desperation.

Never follow the crowd in what you do.
The crowd has never produced anything
of lasting quality, value, or beauty.

Never lose an opportunity of seeing
anything that is beautiful.

A smile is the light in your window
that lets others know there is
a caring person inside.

Success is simply a matter of
luck. Ask any failure.

A problem defined is half-solved.

Be your best today and that will
make you better tomorrow.

If You Think You Can, You Can

You can be a total winner, even if you're a beginner
If you think you can you can, if you think you can
you can You can wear the gold medallion, you
can ride your own black stallion If you think you
can you can, if you think you can you can

It's not your talent or the gifted birth
It's not your bank book that determines worth
It isn't in your gender or the color of your skin
It's your attitude that lets you win

You can live with "coulds" or "shoulds," or be like
Tiger Woods If you think you can you can, if you
think you can you can Even if you're hesitant,
you can be a woman president If you think you
can you can, if you think you can you can

It doesn't matter what you've done before It makes no difference what the halftime score It's never over 'til the final gun So keep on trying and you'll find you've won

Just grab your dream and then believe it Go out and work, and you'll achieve it If you think you can, you can If you think you can, you can

Attitude Is the Edge

At the world-class level, talent is nearly equal. On the PGA Tour only a few strokes for the year separate the top money winners in golf from the rest of the players. In baseball, the American and National League batting champions hit safely about 20 or 30 more times in an entire season than those below the top ten. In the Olympic Games, the difference between the gold-medal winner in the one hundred meter dash and the fourth place, non-medal winner is less than two-tenths of a second.

What's true in sports is also true in our business and personal lives. There is only a fractional difference between winners in life and those who merely exist. The difference is attitude under pressure. It's the winner's edge.

The edge is not a gifted birth. The world is full of wasted talent.

The edge is not academic degrees. Education is important, but the world is full of educated misfits.

The edge is not luck. If it were, Las Vegas would be a ghost town.

The edge is not capital. Many of today's self-made, multi-millionaires started building their fortunes with under $5,000.

The edge is all attitude. Attitude, not aptitude, is the criterion for success.

What you see is who you'll be!

You always project on the outside
how you feel on the inside.

The most important three words
you can say to yourself:
"Yes, I can!"

The most important opinion you'll ever
have is the one you hold of yourself.

Winners believe in their dreams when
that's all they have to hang onto.

When you are able to applaud yourself,
it is much easier to applaud others.

If you believe you can...
you probably can.

If you believe you won't...
you most assuredly won't.

Belief is the ignition switch that
gets you off the launching pad.

Success is a process, not a status. It is a
road that is always under construction.

Seeing Is Believing, or Is It?

When your eyes are open, you see the world that lies outside yourself. You see the items in the room you're in, the people, and the view of the landscape through the window. You take for granted that the objects are real and separate from yourself.

However, successful individuals see the act of achieving in advance— vivid, multi-dimensional, clear. Champions know that, "What you see is who you'll be."

When you close your eyes, images and thoughts flow through your mind. You may review memories of past events, or preview future possibilities. You can daydream about what may be or what might have been, and your imagination will take you beyond the limits of space and time. Most people attach little importance to these inner visions. They may seem pleasantly irrelevant, or uncomfortably at odds with the accepted external reality.

If you're like most people, you grew up with the idea that "seeing is believing." In other words, you need to physically see something with your own eyes to believe that it's real.

I know many successful individuals who live this way.

But there's an attitude that suggests, "Before you can see it, you have to believe it." This premise holds that our belief system is so powerful that thoughts can actually cause things to happen in the physical world.

I also know many successful individuals who live according to this notion of reality.

So which concept is nearer the truth? Do you have to see it before you believe it, or believe before you can see it? The answer is: both are basically true. If you can see something in your mind's eye, and you imagine it over and over again, you will begin to believe it is really there in substance. As a result, your actions, both physical and mental, will move to bring about in reality the image you are visualizing.

During my university years at the U. S. Naval Academy at Annapolis, I underwent training in aircraft recognition. All of us midshipmen sat at one end of a hall while silhouettes of American and foreign military aircraft were flashed on a screen at speeds similar to combat situations. We were supposed to write down the numerical designations and names of the planes, such as A-4, F-ll-F, F-4, MIG-21, and so forth. But the task became more difficult each week, because they kept adding more planes, scrambling the order, and speeding up the projection.

Finally, it got ridiculous, because the images were going by faster than an MTV music video so that most of us saw only a blur, and some didn't see anything. I began to see planes that weren't even invented yet.

When it came time for the final exam, I didn't know for certain which planes I was seeing. I wrote down hunches, intuitions, and reflex responses. But when the test results were announced, virtually everyone had scored a perfect

100 percent. We had seen the planes, even if we didn't necessarily believe it. For me, that test proved that images can be stored and retained, unconsciously, at incredible speeds. And those stored images, when recalled, can enhance performance.

What about the thousands of flickering images we see on a TV, computer, or movie screen? What about commercials? Do we have to believe the products really do all those amazing things before we buy them? Do viewers have to think that violent scenes in movies and TV are actually occurring in real life for there to be a negative effect on their behavior? Many people believe that violent fantasy has no impact on their lives whatsoever, because they think they're too intelligent to be swayed by it.

Well, I've got news for them. Whatever you see or experience, real or imagined, consciously or subliminally, when repeated vividly over and over, does affect your behavior, and definitely can influence you to buy a product or buy into a lifestyle, good or bad. Your attitude and beliefs are, quite simply, functions of what you see day in and day out. Information can be taken in almost unnoticed. You won't react to it until later, and you still won't be aware of what lies behind your response. In other words, what you see really is what you get, regardless of whether you know it or not.

You don't need to be watching slides of airplanes, or TV shows, or music videos, video games, or commercials. You can be just lying down, or commuting to work, or walking through a park, and by seeing from within, in your mind's eye, you can change your life.

By rehashing fears and problems, you can make yourself depressed. As a result you can botch a business deal, hurt a relationship, or lower your performance. By forecasting a gloomy outcome in your mind's eye, you can act as your own witch doctor and practice a modern-day kind of voodoo that will fulfill your negative prediction with uncanny accuracy.

On the other hand, by replaying in your mind's eye the best game you ever played, you can repeat that best game again, when the stakes are even higher and the pressure is on. And by mentally preplaying the best game you've ever imagined, you can set the stage for a world-class performance. This "instant replay" and "instant preplay" applies to anything from a successful sales call or athletic event to the effective motivation of your teammates and children.

Choose your role models and inputs carefully. Your attitudes and beliefs are the software programs driving you every day on life's journey. ⚘

Chapter Three

Seeds of Discipline

EXCELLENCE IS A HABIT

41

Paying the Price

I've studied and counseled many world-class athletes, but no one has inspired me more in recent years than champion cyclist Greg LeMond. Watching him overcome setback after setback during his unparalleled conquest of The Tour de France, I have come to view him as the model for commitment and self-discipline.

Can you remember when you got your first two-wheeler? It's an experience many people can recall instantly. I'll never forget when I got a bicycle for Christmas. My whole family stood on the lawn watching me try to take my first ride. On that day, I discovered why commitment is definitely like riding a bicycle.

First, you must believe that a machine that can't even stand by itself will transport you safely. Of course, you've seen it work for others, but now you've got to convince yourself that this form of success can actually happen to you.

Second, you must let go of all forms of support and balance yourself with the sheer force of momentum and your own strength.

Third, you have to lean into curves. This becomes easy enough after a while, but at the beginning—just as with snow skiing—the natural tendency is to incline yourself away from what appears to be a potentially dangerous situation. You've got to realize that the best way to avoid falling doesn't involve simply staying as far as possible from the ground.

Fourth, you can coast for a while, but you won't get far if you don't keep pedaling. The lesson there, if you've had the privilege of watching Greg LeMond in action, is self-evident.

Last, you've got to get up and try again after you've fallen off the bicycle. Kids will fall any number of times, but they'll almost never say, "I quit. I'm not willing to risk falling again. Forget bicycling. I'd rather just walk or take the bus until I can afford a car." Kids rarely attach any significance to even dozens of falls or failures. Again, we have to watch film clips of Greg LeMond getting up from falls and tragedies time and again to understand that it's the price kids and champions will gladly pay for that marvelous experience of flying down the road or up a mountain under their own power.

This commitment and discipline to "paying the price" is a key quality in the mind of a champion. You could even say that if success has an entry fee, the cost is total commitment through daily discipline.

No train, no gain! Practice does indeed make for permanent performance. 🚲

We learn by observation,
imitation, and repetition.

Your mind can't distinguish reality
from that which has been vividly
and repeatedly imagined.

Habits begin as offhanded remarks,
ideas, and images. And then, layer
upon layer, through practice, they
grow from cobwebs into cables that
shackle or strengthen our lives.

Habits are like submarines.
They run silent and deep.

Habits are rarely broken.
They are replaced.

First we make our habits,
then our habits make us.

Imagination plus internalization
equals realization.

It takes just as much effort to lead a good or a bad life. It all depends on who your role models and mentors are.

Habits are like comfortable beds. They are easy to get into, but difficult to get out of.

Winning and losing are both learned habits.

My Robot: R-U-ME2

I have a little robot
That goes around with me
I tell him what I'm thinking
I tell him what I see
I tell my little robot
All my hopes and fears
He listens and remembers
All my joys and tears
At first my little robot
Followed my command
But after years of training
He's gotten out of hand
He doesn't care what's right or wrong
Or what is false or true
No matter what I try now
He tells me what to do!

Discipline is doing within,
while you do without.

Another name for experience is practice.
Rehearse at every opportunity.

Courage comes easily to those
who are well trained.

Wisdom cannot be inherited. It must
be learned, nurtured, and practiced.

Success is a process, not a status. It's
what you do every day and night.

The Power of Habit

You may know me.
I'm your constant companion.
I'm your greatest helper;
I'm your heaviest burden
I will push you onward or
drag you down to failure.
I am at your command.
Half the tasks you do might as well be turned
over to me. I'm able
to do them quickly, and I'm able to do them
the same every time,
if that's what you want.

I'm easily managed;
all you've got to do is be firm with me.
Show me exactly how you want it done;
after a few lessons
I'll do it automatically.
I am the servant of all great men and women;
of course, I'm the servant
of all the failures as well.
I've made all the winners who have ever
lived. And, I've made all the losers too.

But I work with all the precision of a
marvelous computer with the
intelligence of a human being. You may
run me for profit, or you may run me to
ruin; it makes no difference to me.

Take me. Be easy with me,
and I will destroy you.
Be firm with me,
and I'll put the world at your feet.
Who am I?
I'm Habit![2]

2. Waitley, Denis, *Being the Best* (Nashville, Tennessee: Oliver-Nelson
Books, a division of Thomas Nelson Publishers, 1987), p. 166

Chapter Four

Seeds of Honesty

INTEGRITY IS 24/7

Integrity:
The Real Bottom Line

A simple motto hung on the living room wall of my grandparents' small frame house, where many seeds for my development were planted. My grandmother and grandfather didn't talk about the lines; they lived them.

Life is like a field of newly fallen snow;
where I choose to walk, every step will show.

They believed you were either honest or you weren't. There was nothing in between, no such thing as partial honesty.

Integrity, a standard of personal morality and ethics, is not relative to the situation you happen to find yourself in and doesn't sell out to expediency. Its short supply is getting even shorter—but without it, leadership is a facade.

Learning to see through exteriors is a critical development in the transition from adolescence to adulthood. Sadly, most people continue to be taken in by big talk and media popularity, flashy or bizarre looks, and expensive possessions. They move through most of their years convinced that the externals are what count, and are thus doomed to live shallow lives. Men and women who rely on their looks or status to feel good about themselves inevitably do everything they can to enhance the impression they make—and do correspondingly little to develop their inner value and personal growth. The paradox is that the people who try hardest to impress are often the least impressive. Devotion to image is often for the money it can reap. Puffing to appear powerful is an attempt to hide insecurity. If only we could see many of our celebrities when their guard and pretenses were down!

The myth that all that counts is bottom-line success often leads to fleeting stardom and ultimate defeat. Ask a thousand has-beens. There are no degrees of integrity. You have it or you don't. ❧

Parable for Passing the Buck

This is a story about four people named Everybody, Somebody, Anybody, and Nobody. There was an important job to be done, and Everybody was sure Somebody would do it. Anybody could have done it, but Nobody did it. Somebody got angry about that because it was Everybody's job. Everybody thought Anybody could do it, but Nobody realized that Everybody wouldn't do it. It ended up that Everybody blamed Somebody when Nobody did what Anybody could have done.[3]

---

3. Waitley, Denis, *Being the Best* (Nashville, Tennessee: Oliver-Nelson Books, a division of Thomas Nelson Publishers, 1987), p. 166

The Wax Empire

In the Roman Empire's final corrupt years, status was conveyed by the number of carved statues of the gods displayed in people's courtyards. As in every business, the Roman statue industry had good and bad sculptors and merchants. As the empire became ever more greedy and narcissistic, the bad got away with as much as they could. Sculptors became so adept at using wax to hide cracks and chips in marble that most people couldn't discern the difference in quality. Statues began to weep or melt under the scrutiny of sunlight or heat in foyers.

For statues of authentic fine quality, carved by reputable artists, people had to go to the artisan marketplace in the Roman Quad and look for booths with signs declaring *sine cera* (without wax). We too look for the real thing in friends, products, and services. In people, we value sincerity—from *sine cera*—more than almost any other virtue. We should expect it from our leaders. We must demand it of ourselves.

Integrity that strengthens an inner value system is the real human bottom line. Commitment to a life of integrity in every situation demonstrates that your word is more valuable than a surety bond. It means you don't base your decisions on being politically correct. You do what's right, not what's fashionable. You know that truth is absolute, not a device for manipulating others. And you win in the long run, when the stakes are highest. ❦

You must consider the bottom line,
but make it integrity before profit.

My Personal Code of Self Respect

I am valuable because I was created with an inner value and worth. I do not have to earn it.

I improve my self respect when I understand and accept that I have basic inner value. The value is there. I don't have to achieve it. I already have it. My challenge is to nurture and protect my inner value from getting jaded or twisted by the misplaced values of a success-at-any-cost oriented society.

If I can avoid the trap of trying to possess success or adorn myself with success at the expense of others, I can easily acquire self respect. It is important for me to do things that project my inner value to other people.

I understand that integrity is a 24-hours-a-day, 7-days-a-week character trait. It is non-situational, not a convenience.

I realize that integrity is doing what's right, even though that decision may not give me immediate pleasure or ease my present burden.

My worth is my word. I make commitments, and I do what I say I will do. This is more than important to me—it is crucial.

I say to others: "I am valuable, as you are valuable. We will make a value exchange. I will offer you the best I have, and I trust you will give me your best in return.

I prefer to be a role model worth emulating by my children and their children, than have the applause of the masses. Integrity cannot be overshadowed by celebrity. ❧

Your Investment Portfolio

The dictionary defines integrity in terms of soundness of moral character, adherence to ethical principles, and being unimpaired. Its middle English root is related to integrate—to bring together into a whole—and integral—complete, whole. Another relative is the mathematical integer, a whole number, not a fraction. These references to wholeness rightly suggest that integrity affects all aspects of our lives, which is why I like to refer to it as a healthy investment portfolio filled with blue chip stocks such as honesty, fairness, loyalty, courtesy, cooperation, compassion, generosity, and kindness.

What can we do to increase the dwindling integrity in our society today? Like charity, integrity begins at home. One of the greatest gifts you can give your children is a strong sense of ethical and moral values. Let them accept responsibility for their own actions as early as possible. The more sense of responsibility they develop, the better they will feel about themselves.

Above all, for integrity's sake, teach them graciousness and gratitude and how to care about the rights and welfare of others. Teach your children (and business associates who look to you for leadership) that their true rewards in life will depend on the quality and amount of service they render. Show them, by example, how to treat others as they would have others treat them.

If I were writing a single commandment for leadership it would be: "You shall conduct yourself in such a manner as to set an example worthy of imitation by your children and subordinates." In simpler terms, if they shouldn't be doing it, neither should you.

When I told my kids to clean their rooms, for example, they took a closer look at the condition of my tools and possessions in the garage. When I told them that honesty was our family's greatest virtue, they commented on the radar detector I had installed in my car. When I told them about the vices of drinking and wild parties, they watched from the upstairs balcony the way our guests behaved at our adult functions.

Integrity is easier preached than practiced. We go along for a while setting a good example, but sometimes we tell ourselves we need a break. The trouble is, our children and subordinates get confused. First they think we are being ourselves by modeling healthy behavior. When they see the unhealthy behavior coming from their leaders, they are puzzled and hurt at first, but then they catch on. They learn to play the game of "say one thing, do another." The old cliché holds true: What you are speaks so loudly no one can really hear what you say. But it is even more true that if what you are matches what you say, your life will speak forcefully indeed.

It's hardly a secret that learning ethical standards begins at home. A child's first inklings of a sense of right and wrong come from almost imperceptible signals received long before he or she reaches the age of rational thought about morality. Maybe you're asking yourself what kind of model you are for future generations, remembering that people are either honest or dishonest, that integrity is all or nothing, and that children can't be fooled in such basic matters. They learn by example. ⚘

I'd Rather Watch a Winner

I'd rather watch a winner, than hear one any day
So please my loving parents let your
lives show me the way

I'm only a reflection of what you taught today
I may misunderstand you and the high advice
you give But there's no misunderstanding
how you act and how you live

So teach me by example, don't preach about what's right
And show me by your actions every day and night
I know that you're not perfect, in
the things you do and say

And the lectures you deliver are to help me find my way
But I'd rather watch a winner, than hear one any day[4]

---

4. Waitley, Denis, *Seeds of Greatness* (Old Tappan, New Jersey: Fleming H. Revell Company, 1983) p. 209

Success is not so much what we have, as it is what we are.

You are your own scriptwriter and the play is never finished, no matter what your age or position in life.

Success is working harder or smarter—usually both— doing what you enjoy and are good at.

The trouble with reading your own press clippings is that you start to believe them.

The most important conversations
you'll ever have are the conversations
you have with yourself.

If you have real, internal value, you
don't need a loud, expensive imitation.

It is not what you get that makes
you successful, it is what you are
continuing to do with what you've got.

When you are talking to yourself,
watch your language!

Individuals with good self-esteem
can accept or reject the opinions of
others, but never depend on them
for your sense of worthiness.

Identify with excellence, put your name
on your work, and both your work and
name will stand the test of time.

The Integrity Triad

One of the principles of integrity is to defend your convictions in the face of great social pressure. Consider this true story about an abdominal surgery performed in a large, well-known hospital. It was the surgical nurse's first day on the medical team. Responsible for ensuring that all instruments and materials were accounted for before completing the operation and sewing up the incision, she told the surgeon that he had removed only eleven sponges. "We used twelve and we need to find the last one," she reported. "No, I removed them all," the doctor declared emphatically. "We'll close the incision now." "No," the rookie nurse objected, "we used twelve sponges." "I'll take the responsibility," the surgeon said grimly. "Suture, please." "You can't do that, sir," blazed the nurse. "Think of the patient!" The surgeon lifted his foot, revealing where he had hidden the twelfth sponge. "You'll do just fine in this or any other hospital," he said, smiling.

Don't back down when you know you're right.

A second key integrity principle is always to give others the credit that's rightfully theirs, never fearing anyone who has a better idea or is smarter than you.

David Ogilvy, founder of Ogilvy and Mather, made this point to newly appointed office heads by sending them a matryoshka, the painted Russian doll with five progressively smaller dolls nestled inside. His message to his new executives was in the smallest doll: "If we hire people who are smaller than we are, we'll become a company of dwarves. But if each of us hires people bigger than we are, we'll become a company of giants." And that is precisely what Ogilvy and Mather became, one of the world's largest and most respected advertising firms.

Look up to those beneath you.

Our third integrity principle is to be honest and open about who you really are. Be yourself. Don't exaggerate your achievements. Don't get trapped in a cover-up of past mistakes, even of personal traits that dissatisfy or displease you. When the going is tough, be tough by facing reality with adult responses. Use the good and the bad as material for personal growth.

Accept responsibility for your decisions.

Is integrity a primary consideration in a practical, profit-making organization? Not to have it courts the risk of sophisticated surveillance equipment, disgruntled employees, and IRS tipsters. Ethics deprivation can lead to inner rot. The company building may be located in a high-rent district. It may be made of the finest steel, chrome, and glass—but it will decay from the inside.

Can you think of a successful relationship without integrity? I doubt it. All are based on mutual trust. Break that trust and you break the relationship. Subvert it and it's almost impossible to put together again. Creating a long-term relationship takes two or more people—whether executives, representatives of labor and management, parent and child, or husband and wife who are grounded in and operating on the same non-situational integrity. Nothing less will last.

When *Fortune* magazine asked the CEOs of many Fortune 500 companies what they considered the most important qualities for hiring and promoting top executives, the unanimous consensus was that integrity and trustworthiness were by far the key qualities. That survey of leading businessmen—not of preachers or motivational speakers—speaks for itself.

Here are some tips to help you further embrace integrity in your personal, business, and family life:

1. Justice and fair play are integrity's core values. Go out of your way to be helpful and make others number one in your life. A smile will almost always be returned with a smile—and you're none the worse for the wear even if it's not.

2. Set high standards of ethics for yourself and expect others to do the same. Your single most powerful teaching

tool is not talking about what's right but quietly doing it. A businessperson or a parent who lectures about obeying the rules but constantly breaks them is making an especially powerful negative statement. The old "Do as I say, not as I do" is severely damaging to children and subordinates.

3. Give of your best in the worst of times. Personal integrity knows no season and doesn't hinge on the weather, the stock market report, or the leading economic indicators. You have it or you don't.

4. As my friend Dr. Ted Engstrom advises in his book *Integrity*, chart your course by the north star of conscience by doing unto others as you would have them do unto you. Most of the world's religions have long urged the same. "Do not to others what you would not want done to you" is a pillar of ancient Chinese philosophy. Charting your course by the north star means you are stable, constant, resolute. You base your decisions on principle, on your immovable belief system.

5. Respect diversity in culture and heritage. The world's rapid transportation, interactive media, virtual reality, and global communications network means we must learn to live in harmony with other human beings. The dictionary tells us that integrity is wholeness, which implies mutual acceptance. Don't make the futile attempt of trying to be an island. Welcome the

foreigner. Work hard at understanding other cultures, languages, and points of view.

6. Read articles and books about integrity and make your car a university on wheels by listening to CDs and tapes of self-improvement and business programs. Be willing to be stretched in your thinking. What would you do if you found a wallet with a good deal of money in it? Adults are often confronted by much more serious problems. Ask yourself if you have the solid, bedrock values to get you through any situation without compromise.

Your children and subordinates will do what they see you do. Your challenge as a leader is enormous, but so are the rewards. A life of principle—of not succumbing to the temptations of immediate gratification—will always win in the end, leading you to the real wealth of a clear conscience and not having to constantly check the rear view mirror as you move forward. ⚘

Look Inside

When the prize seems high above you
And your mirror doesn't love you
Look inside

When the road to gold gets steeper
And your diamond's buried deeper
Look inside

Light a candle in your mind
Untold riches you will find
When you look for treasures
Look inside

When you're running low on laughter
And can't reach the goals you're after
Look inside

When your body starts complaining
And the clouds of doubt keep raining
Look inside

Close your eyes and then believe it
Trust yourself and you'll achieve it
When you're seeking answers
Look inside

Chapter Five

Seeds of Confidence

VALUE IS INSIDE OUT

Core Values:
From Inside to Outside

Core values radiate like rings, as when a leaf falls in a pond. The self-centered constantly seek approval from and power over others. They try to impress them with their worth rather than express concern for others' well-being. And their outward appearances usually involve ways to hide their real thoughts and intentions.

The paradoxical proverb here is that:

You must feel worthy of the best,
but not more worthy than the rest.

The value-centered give of themselves freely and graciously, constantly seeking to empower others. Open and modest, they have no need for conceit, the opposite of core value. Feeling good about who they are, and not needing to talk about their victories or line their walls with celebrity photos, people with core values spend much of their time "paying value," as I call it, to others. When praised, they share the spotlight. When they make mistakes, they view them as learning experiences and accept responsibility.

My friend Nathaniel Branden has taught me—and countless others—that self-esteem can't be bought, won in an arena, measured by a stock portfolio, or displayed in a fashion model's figure or an entertainment star's profile.

Self-esteem is a profound belief that you deserve to be happy and successful, combined with a trust or confidence in an ability to manage life's challenges. It is as necessary for human development as oxygen, as basic as the carbon from which diamonds are formed. I used to think that diamonds were so sought after because they glitter, but discovered that they're actually so valuable because they're almost impossible to destroy. Formed at the earth's core and very rare, they hold their value indefinitely.

Perhaps you have already developed the wisdom to know that the diamonds you seek are waiting to be uncovered in your own back yard—the back yard of your mind—where your sense of values and your self-worth are embedded.

The simple truth is that if we have no internalized feelings of value, we have nothing to share with others. We can need them, depend on them, look for security in them—but we can't share or give an emotion to anyone unless we possess it. The diamond is inside us, waiting to be discovered, shaped, and polished. ⛏

Here are some action tips to enhance your self-esteem and that of the significant others in your life:

1. Be more aware of your physical appearance. You don't have to be the best-looking in any group, just look your best. Being clean says you care about yourself. Make a commitment to join a support group with a proven program that will overcome any habit that reduces the quality of your life.

2. Improve your body language. Stand erect yet relaxed. Walk purposefully but without arrogance. Your jaw and face should be relaxed, your eyes bright and in direct contact with others while in conversation, your pronunciation should be clear, your voice projecting confidence and intensity. Always extend your hand and offer your own name first in any personal encounter— and offer your name first in phone conversations. Smile with your eyes, voice, face, and body language. In every language, a smile is a light in your window that says a caring person resides within.

3. In your day planner, whether it's in electronic format or on paper, write down and define the success qualities you want to acquire. Help your associates and family members do the same. You may want to focus on one quality a month. It takes about a month of repetition to

develop a new habit, about a year of practice to make it permanent.

4. Make a thanks list. Write "I am thankful for the following" at the top of a page, then three columns for People, Things, and Other. List all the people and things for which you are grateful. In the Other column, consider items we tend to take for granted, such as freedom, health, and opportunity. Read your list twice a day for a week and discuss it with associates and significant family members. When disappointment clamors for attention, review your blessings and your thanks list. Teach the members of your team to like what they have rather than constantly trying to have what they like.

5. Dwell on your strengths and talents. Keep a video record of your professional and personal milestones and achievements—positive memories for reinforcement during difficult times. Also, make a video of the older members of your family and senior members of your company relating their experiences and expertise. Nothing is more important to rookies and the younger generation than wisdom from people who have been there before. And nothing is more important than featuring dedicated employees who may not be getting the attention they deserve.

6. Communicate unconditional acceptance of yourself and significant others regardless of their current performance. When criticizing specific behavior, be certain

to reassure your associates and children of your love. A core of self-acceptance is a powerful defense against needing externals to define self-esteem.

7. Become comfortable giving and receiving compliments and expressions of affection. An ability to accept appreciation is a sign of healthy self-esteem.

8. Be open to criticism and relaxed about acknowledging your mistakes. Your self-esteem is not tied to being always right or to an image of perfection.

9. Since you trust your ability to cope with challenge and change, enjoy life's ironies and humorous aspects. Remain flexible in your responses, eager to contribute inventiveness and innovation.

10. Make the first and last fifteen minutes of your day at home and at the office—the time I call sign-on and sign-off signatures—the most important for all around you. Make it a habit, no less important than brushing your teeth, to start your day on a positive note. Wake up looking forward to a new slate. Send your partner, child, or spouse off with a loving, encouraging thought. Send yourself off to work with a bright outlook. Send everyone at your factory or office forward with the expected results, not the morning newspaper's bad news. Just as important, use the last fifteen minutes of your office and family day to let others know how much you care for them—by signing off with a reassuring,

optimistic sentence or two. Just before leaving the office, think of something in your working environment that brings you satisfaction and pass it on. Do the same at home before going to sleep. I believe this has influenced my family to rise higher in their aspirations. I know it has changed my own life. ⚘

Coming Home
(Dedicated to POWs and Refugees)

It takes courage to say what you want to
And to believe in the things that you choose
But having a home to belong to
Is the greatest of freedoms to lose

When you're away from home
You get to wondering
Why you are where you are and whatever
Made you go so far
And when you're alone at night
You start remembering
That someone is lonely too
And they mean more than life to you
And you want to come home

And when your tears come down
Just like falling rain
And you want so much to feel a touch
To ease your pain
And there in your emptiness
You start to pray
Please let me see their face
And feel the warmth of their embrace
Because there's no place like home

And when you return you'll know
You'll never want to roam
And you'll be truer to those close to you
And you'll let them know
You'll never give away another day
And you'll be free again, to be you again
When you finally come home
Because there's no place like home
And you're coming home

The greatest limitations you will ever
face will be those you place on yourself.

You always project on the outside
how you feel on the inside.

Expect the best, plan for the worst,
and prepare to be surprised.

You can only do good if you feel good.

Don't let negative people
determine your self-worth.

The price of success is to bear
the criticism of envy.

The more you know, the
less you need to say.

The most important labels in society
are the ones we hang on ourselves.

The stretch of the limousine usually
is inversely proportional to the self-
esteem of the person riding in it.

Nice guys finish best!

This I Believe

I believe in myself.

I believe that all people have the equal right to become all they are willing and able to become.

I believe that I am as good as anyone in the world. Although I may never be on the cover of *Time* or *People* magazine—I still have time to be one of the people who makes a really positive difference in the world.

I believe that although I may not be the best looking in the group, I'll always be looking my best in every group!

I believe in this and the next generation, and believe we'll build a better nation.

I believe that good health means more than wealth.

I believe in caring and sharing, rather than comparing.

I believe of all the people I see, still I'd rather be me!

Chapter Six

Seeds of Love

THE ULTIMATE GIFT

Love: Unconditional Acceptance and Trust

There are many definitions and interpretations of love. I've always looked at love as unconditional acceptance and "looking for the good." Perhaps one of the best and most appropriate descriptions of love is that given by Dr. Gerald Jampolsky, a well-known psychiatrist, author, and founder of the Center for Attitudinal Healing in Tiburon, California. Dr. Jampolsky teaches children and adults experiencing emotional and physical crises that "love is letting go of fear."

With love, there can be no fear. Love is natural and unconditional. Love asks no questions—neither preaching nor demanding; neither comparing nor measuring; Love is—pure and simple—the greatest value of all. And, most importantly, we must feel love inside ourselves before we can give it to others.

Simple, isn't it? If there is no deep, internal feeling of value inside us, then we have nothing to give to or share with others. We can need them, we can be dependent upon them, we can look for security in them, we can indulge them, flatter them, and attempt to purchase them. But we cannot share or give an emotion to anyone else, unless we first have that emotion inside ourselves.

Love is not fulfilling our expectations through someone else. Love is not possessing another person to make us whole. Love is giving and sharing. It is the ultimate expression of the double win.

This concern about holding on to or possessing love is how many relationships are perceived, pursued, and destroyed. Love is an expression of the value we place on a person independent of his or her ability to meet our needs. Authentic love makes you want to set your partner free, not possess him or her.

In my own relationships, I like to think I'm more liberating than possessive, that I'm rarely captured by envy or jealousy, and that I tend to give without worrying about what I might get in return. But I'm as far from perfect as everyone else. Sometimes I sense that my tendency to be a good Samaritan nurturer comes from a need for approval. Trying to share my values out of love is one thing. Seeking approbation in order to neutralize the fear of abandonment that may have sprung from my childhood in a broken home is another—and I can't always be certain of my ultimate motive. How about you? Do you help others so they can fly free or in hopes that they'll approve of you? Of course, human motives are almost always mixed, but the constant is that the best way to ensure you are loved by those important to you is to empower them to become as independent and valuable as they can be. The proverb is:

You must strive to be lovable, but
not desperate to be loved.

Only when you set your romantic partner free to be all he or she can be will you know how attractive and lovable you are yourself, free of the insecurity and self-doubt that spawn envy and jealousy.

When others sense you have their interests rather than only your own at heart, they begin to trust you. That foundation of all friendships and healthy marriages is also the key to customer service and satisfaction. You never just close a sale. What you do is open a long-term relationship based on mutual disclosure and mutual trust. ❧

Love for All Creatures Great and Small

My friend Georglyn owned a Yorkshire Terrier I'll always remember. He was a cute little fellow, with beautiful long hair that needed to be brushed every day. Actually, Buckwheat didn't really belong to my friend; he belonged to their daughter Natalie.

When Natalie and her parents moved into a new home in Mesa, Arizona, they put in a swimming pool to take advantage of the climate. They planted what was to be a lush, green lawn around the pool and installed underground sprinklers. Buckwheat couldn't keep his nose out of anything. He kept falling into the pool and would either climb out or have to be fished out. Then he would shake furiously to dry off and roll in the fertilizer on top of the new lawn. When Natalie tried to brush his matted hair, he would yelp and snap at her.

Every day Buckwheat explored his new domain. Whenever the sprinklers popped up automatically, catching him off guard, he would chase and bite the spray from these "invaders," barking incessantly to warn the family. When Natalie's brother, Nathan, cleaned the pool, the long hose thrashed back and forth like a fire hose with no one holding on. Buckwheat came to the rescue and charged valiantly into the water, growling and biting the enemy.

After the battle he would roll in the fertilizer again. His tangled, mud-encrusted coat was beyond repair and his smell led him to become an outdoor dog for the day. Later, at the dog grooming clinic, the prognosis was as the family had feared—Buckwheat's hair would have to go! It took three people to hold him down during the operation, which consisted of shaving him almost to the skin.

The reception back home was not what little Buckwheat had expected, after all he'd been subjected to. When he was carried indoors, the other kids—Leah and Halie—laughed and made fun of him because he didn't look like a beautiful "Yorkie" any more. He looked more like a giant rat from a science fiction movie in which nature gets her revenge on technology, with a strange mutation.

Buckwheat reacted to the teasing by hiding under the living-room sofa. Instead of jumping onto everyone's lap, licking every available face, he cowered out of sight. When he finally found it necessary to get food or water, he sneaked behind the couch and chairs to his dish after the family had left the dining area. He sat in a corner of the house for two days, shivering uncontrollably when anyone came near him. It took several days of constant loving, holding, and stroking by the family before he was convinced that he was still accepted.

I tell this story because it taught all of us a crucial lesson. When Buckwheat lost his beautiful coat he lost more than beauty. The derisive laughter told him that he no longer belonged. His shivering was not caused primarily by the cold; he felt afraid, alone, and rejected. In short, Buck-wheat's self-esteem plunged to zero. His fearful trembling was not that different from the cowering of thousands of human beings who are hiding in the shadows of rejection. And Buckwheat's recovery of good self-esteem—accomplished only with much stroking and caring—illustrates perfectly the most precious gift that can be given or received: the gift of love. 🐦

You Need Someone to Love You

When you're staring in the mirror
and you don't like who you see
When you think you're not good
looking like the actors on TV
When there's always someone brighter
and more talented than you
It's pretty hard to ever think your
own dreams can come true

When you're there in the arena,
watching champions go for gold
And you cheer them on to victory
and world records they can hold
When you do the wave there in
the stands, just wishing it was you
It's pretty hard to ever think your
own dreams can come true

That's why you need someone to love you,
why you need someone to care; who gives you
courage to hang onto and urges you to dare

That's why you need someone who trusts you
Who shares that dream you see
Who lifts you up when you are down
And that someone is me.

Like a gentle wind beneath you
so your wings can spread and fly
With my arms wrapped strong around you
when you feel like you could cry
With me right there in your corner
when you're fighting for what's right
And my faith and love to guide you
when the darkness hides the light

When you're staring in the mirror
then you'll smile at who you see
And you'll feel more self-esteem
than all those actors on TV
When there's someone who is there
for you in everything you do
It's pretty hard not to believe your
own dreams will come true

That's why you need someone to love you,
why you need someone to care; who gives you
courage to hang onto and urges you to dare

That's why you need someone who trusts you
Who shares that dream you see
Who lifts you up when you are down
And that someone is me.

Love and Marriage

Commitment to a single partner offers the greatest potential for a win-win life. It combines the natural self-ishness of wanting another person to fulfill longed-for fantasies with the chance to be your vulnerable self, able to reveal your innermost thoughts.

One of the most meaningful non-fiction books I ever read is the little-known *Me: The Narcissistic American* by Aaron Stern, a psychiatrist who served as an educational consultant to the United Nations and as a director of the Motion Picture Association of America's Code and Rating Administration. It zeroes in brilliantly on the greatest cause of America's social problems: our narcissistic preoccupation with immediate gratification.

Dr. Stern's understanding of marriage is especially rich. It should, he says, combine "the exquisite excitement of adolescent romance with the ability to assume the responsibility involved in caring for each other. The absence of either of these qualities makes the relationship incomplete. Together they sharpen the sense of fulfillment loving gives us." Dr. Stern believes that every marriage needs some adolescent love as a spice to keep romance alive. But spice is properly added for flavor, not to overwhelm the main course.

In our relationships with our significant others, we can too easily become preoccupied with professional goals, financial matters, and family responsibilities. We need to recapture our longing to play hide-and-seek, to dine and dance in candlelight, to walk on the beach as we did in our courtship. We need to do more walking and less talking about schedules. We need to rediscover being more spontaneous and less structured. We need to touch each other and listen to music more, take more evening swims, and light more fires in the fireplace. We need more romantic getaways and fewer business trips. We need to experience each other without constant interruption, and to set aside more time without phones, e-mails, meetings, children, or even friends.

Just as it takes effort to nurture children to become independent and to empower employees to assume responsibility, it takes real effort to bolster your commitment to your life partner. Healthy love can't be demanded nor taken for granted. It can only be a continuing give-and-take exchange and dialogue between two independent persons who share many values and responsibilities, yet still feel a childlike magic with each other. Love returns when it is set free. 🌱

Love is unconditional acceptance
and looking for good.

You must feel love within,
before you can share it.

Love should be a verb, not a noun or
adverb. Love is an active emotion.

If you want to be loved, first be lovable.

Value is in the doer, not the deed.

Love yourself and give away
all the love you can today.

Self-esteem is based on the
internalization of spiritual love.

Love is one of the few experiences in life
that we can best keep by giving it away.

Touch is the magic wand of intimacy.
Love is keeping in touch.

Love is an expression of the value we
place on a person, independent of his
or her ability to meet our needs.

Authentic love makes you want to set
your partner free, not possess him or her.

And only when you set your romantic
and business partners free to be
all they can be, will you know how
attractive and lovable you are yourself;
free of the insecurity and self-doubt
that spawn envy and jealousy.

To love is to be open and vulnerable, and to receive graciously that which is given.

Don't assume that money, shelter, and creature comforts are enough to demonstrate your love. Nothing can replace your presence, your hug, your smile, your touch—you!

Listening without bias or distraction is the greatest compliment you can pay another person.

Healthy love can't be demanded nor taken for granted. It can only be a continuing give-and-take exchange and dialogue between two independent persons who share many values and responsibilities, yet still feel a childlike magic with each other.

Be willing to set free those to whom you want to cling, even though you risk losing them. Love usually returns when it is free to fly.

The first words you should speak to the one beside you when you awaken each morning are, "Good morning, I love you." The last words you should speak each night are, "Good night, I love you."

Love: The Greatest Four-letter Word

L—is for Listen.

To love someone is to listen unconditionally to his or her values and needs without prejudice.

O—is for Overlook.

To love someone is to overlook the flaws and faults in favor of looking for the good.

V—is for Voice.

To love someone is to voice your approval on a regular basis. There is no substitute for honest encouragement, positive strokes, and praise.

E—is for Effort.

To love someone is to make a constant effort to spend the time, to make the sacrifice, to show your interest.

Chapter Seven

Seeds of Optimism

THE BIOLOGY OF HOPE

Getting High on Your Expectations

Optimism is an incurable condition in the person with faith. Optimists believe that most disease, distress, dysfunction, and disturbance can be cured. Optimists also are prevention oriented. Their thoughts and activities are focused on wellness, health, and success.

It was a Saturday in November and Arnold Lemerand was taking a stroll. He heard some children screaming and hurried over to where they had been playing near a construction site. A massive cast-iron pipe had become dislodged and had rolled down on top of the children, pinning five-year-old Philip Toth against the earth. The boy's head was being forced into the dirt directly under the huge pipe and certain suffocation appeared to be imminent.

Arnold Lemerand looked around but there was no one to help him in the attempted rescue. He did the only thing he could. He reached down and lifted the 1,800-pound, cast-iron pipe off Philip's head. After the incident, he tried again to lift the pipe and could not even budge it. His grown sons tried to move it, but they failed as well.

In an interview later with the Associated Press, Mr. Lemerand, who was 56 at the time, said that he had suffered a major heart attack six years before. "I try to avoid heavy lifting," he smiled, with the young boy's arms around his neck.

We read about such miraculous power surges every so often, don't we? We hear of grandmothers lifting cars and firemen making impossible rescues in burning buildings, exhibiting superhuman strength. Those kinds of stories used to sound rather tall to me, since I've always been a man to check the source and document the advice that people give me as to its validity.

As my life has progressed, I have become a real believer. I don't mean a believer in the sense of a religious faith; I received that faith nearly forty years ago at ten thousand feet, in the cockpit of a private plane I was flying with Louis Evans, Jr. He was the pastor our La Jolla Presbyterian Church at the time. I've always been a positive thinker, but in recent decades I have participated in scientific research and have become a real believer in optimism and what it can do.

I began to learn about how the mind can affect the body and how our thoughts can give us a natural high or make us ill. I was in Sarasota, Florida, serving as president of the International Society for Advanced Education, a non-profit foundation formed by Dr. Jonas Salk and other leading health scientists to study preventive medicine and a holistic approach to wellness. The society was sponsoring continuing medical education seminars in co-operation with the University of Pittsburgh, the University of Nebraska, Johns Hopkins University, Harvard University, and other medical schools.

At some of the seminars many years ago, presenters described research documenting the existence of substances in our brains similar to morphine and heroin. Over thirty years ago they located receptor areas in the brain which act as "locks" that only these unknown substances would fit, like "keys." It was discovered that our brains contained these "keys" in the form of natural hormones. Several have been identified including enkephalin, endorphin, beta-endorphin, and dynorphin. All of these hormones serve as natural pain relievers many times more powerful than morphine. Beta-endorphin is one hundred and ninety times more potent than morphine.

Scientists already knew that hormones play an important role in regulating certain of our biological processes. Adrenalin is the hormone that enables us to "fight or flee," in the face of danger or in response to a call for peak physical performance. Insulin regulates the sugar levels in our blood. Now these later discoveries have proven that morphine-like hormones are being manufactured in our own bodies to block pain and give us a "natural high."

In one test, using endorphin supplied by The Salk Institute, Japanese researchers injected minute amounts of the hormone into fourteen men and women suffering intense pain from cancer. From a single injection, they all felt relief from their pain for one to three days. In another experiment, fourteen expectant mothers were given endorphin during labor. All reported immediate and lasting pain relief and delivered normal babies.

You've heard of the "vicious cycle" in which one problem gives way to another problem, leading back to the first problem. Negative thinking deprives the body of endorphins, leading to depression, leading back to more negative thinking.

Now, let's reverse the process. There is growing scientific evidence that positive mental attitudes and beliefs actually create a natural "high" to help the individual withstand pain, overcome depression, turn stress into energy, and gather strength to persevere. Physical exercise also aids in this process.

In one related study, actors were wired to electrodes and connected to blood catheters. They were then asked to perform various scenes. When they portrayed characters who were angry or depressed or without hope, endorphin levels dropped. But when the scene called for emoting joy, confidence, and love, endorphins shot up.

If our thoughts can cause the brain to release adrenalin from the adrenal glands to help a 56-year-old heart attack patient lift an 1,800-pound pipe off a boy's head; and if our thoughts can produce natural endorphins (even when we are acting out roles) that are fifty to one hundred and ninety times as powerful as morphine, is it not possible for us to use this power of optimism in our everyday lives, with the only side effect being happiness?

When people ask me why I'm so optimistic and high on life, I tell them, "I'm on endorphins." They say, "It figures. We knew you were on something." ✺

Success is not the destination,
it's a way of traveling.

You become that to which
you are most exposed.

Life is a self-fulfilling prophecy. You
may not get what you want, but in the
long run you will get what you expect.

A good life is a collection
of happy memories.

The good old days are here and now!

Choose a career you love and
you'll never have to go to work.

Happiness is the experience of living
a life you feel is worthwhile.

Expect the best from yourself
and others too!

To be enthused is to be infused with life!

Inspire others to do more than they
thought possible of themselves.

Larry's Temporary Inconvenience

Even more of an incurable optimist than Greg LeMond— who has come back from life-threatening cancer to tie the record for most consecutive Tour de France victories—is my friend Larry Robb.

When I first met Larry in the late 1960s he was one of the most successful stockbrokers in Texas. I met him in my hometown of La Jolla, California and we hit it off right away. He was about as positive a thinker and doer as you could ever imagine. Larry was good looking, with a great sense of humor, incisive mind, earning well over six figures a year (and that was nearly forty years ago), and to top it off he had a lovely wife and family. What more could a guy ask for?

Larry and I were flying from Dallas to San Diego one winter day and were discussing his uncanny ability to make money in a crazy stock market. When I asked him his secret, he sounded more like Will Rogers than a modern day whiz kid. "I buy them low and sell them just before they peak or as they peak," he offered.

"What happens if they don't go up or if they peak and fall off the cliff?" "I stay out of those deals," he winked. I told him I would like to make some of that big, quick money, the way he did. He told me that if I would give him one thousand dollars to invest, he would give me three thousand dollars in six months. He got a little bolder and told me to invest four thousand dollars with him which he would convert into ten thousand dollars in twelve months. I sheepishly asked what he could do with four hundred dollars. We laughed and agreed that it wouldn't even pay for my family to go skiing for one week at Lake Tahoe. We both loved to ski and fish and I envied the fact that he was on his way to Montana the following week for a long-awaited trip.

I didn't hear about the plane crash until a week after it had happened. The private aircraft had burned fiercely after impact and Larry had suffered third-degree burns over most of his body. He told me later that he had a choice to make as he was lying in the deep snow. Should he lie there peacefully and let nature take its course or should he try to get up and somehow find help? His surgeon told me later that the severity of his burns gave him a one-in-a-thousand chance of living.

Optimism never ceases to amaze me. Larry remembered the name of Dr. Charles H. Williams, Chief of Anesthesiology at St. Joseph's Hospital in Houston, and called him. Dr. Williams notified Dr. Thomas Biggs, a friend of Larry's and a leading reconstructive surgeon, also in Houston. Dr. Biggs stayed on the telephone during the next several hours, giving instructions as to how to mix and administer the exact proportions of critical body fluids that would keep Larry alive. Dr. Williams flew to Montana in a chartered Learjet and returned Larry to Houston, racing against the clock. It was touch and go for several weeks.

My first personal contact with Larry after his accident was by telephone. I'll never, in my life, forget what he said to me when he answered the phone at his bedside.

"Is that you, Denis?" I heard a familiar tone with a different enunciation.

"How are you doing, Larry?" I asked haltingly.

"I'm doing great, pal," the voice in my receiver said, "I've had a little, temporary inconvenience here that has slowed me down for a while, but no problem!"

I swallowed the waver in my voice and told him he was in my prayers and that I'd check back with him soon. A few months had passed before I called again. I felt guilty for having sent cards instead of personally contacting him. Here was a good friend, lying near death, and I was too busy to try to bring some encouragement into his sterile world. His conversation nearly knocked me off my chair.

"I can talk a little more clearly now," he said. "The scar tissue that was forming around my mouth has been removed surgically. I'm finally back at work. I've set up my office here in the hospital with an incoming and outgoing phone line, so I can sell on one line and still get incoming calls on the other."

All I could do was ask him how business was going. He told me it was a little slow, because now he was selling on sheer ability; whereas during his initial calls most of his business had come as the result of pity.

"I knew the pity wouldn't last more than a couple of weeks," he chuckled. "I've learned to chart the trends, since I can't sell stocks anymore by my good looks alone." As uncomfortable as it felt, I found myself laughing with Larry.

By the time I saw Larry in person, he had endured more than sixty operations and there were many more to come. Even after a year, it was very difficult to look my buddy square in the face. He had been burned much more severely than I had anticipated. But to hear him talk about it, you would have thought he'd burned his fingers barbecuing in the backyard! I went to the therapist with him and watched him go through the excruciating pain of having his fingers pulled, bent, and massaged so he could move them properly and get the tendons stretching back in the right direction.

When he saw me hesitate to talk face to face, he said, "Don't worry, it's still me inside... just a temporary construction job going on at the surface." He told me that if you had faith and really knew yourself from the "inside out," you wouldn't get discouraged when something unexpected came along to threaten you from the "outside in." He said it was difficult for the people in his hometown to deal with his condition. To make it easier for the public, while he was going through the painful skin grafts and plastic reconstruction, he wore a ski mask over his face in restaurants, banks, and stores. "They still laughed and stared at me," he reflected, "but it was more curiosity than revulsion as it had been before. Besides," he went on, "the ski mask got me

motivated to get myself back in shape to hit the ski slopes!"
I wondered how the bank tellers reacted the first time they
saw him walk in with his ski mask on.

Here was a young man, with everything going for him,
when suddenly his world literally went up in smoke. Why
was he not crushed and broken? I thought about the
thousands of young people who take their lives every year
because they are depressed about their inability to cope
with change. I thought about the thousands of complaints
I have heard in my life from people who are just plain
miserable. I thought that since misery loves company, the
reason many people gripe so much about the conditions in
their world is because they, subconsciously, want to bring
the rest of us down to their own miserable level.

Larry proudly showed me the way the doctors had
rebuilt his legs. They had grafted layers of skin tissue from
other parts of his body to his calves and thighs. Although
he was still walking with the aid of a stick when I first saw
him, he soon discarded it as he built his leg strength back
after hours and hours of bicycle riding.

Flying back to San Diego after visiting Larry those many
years ago, I remember staring out of my window and trying
to comprehend his unbelievable attitude. He figured that
if you were born in despair, it would be tough to maintain
your optimism. But his belief was that since he had been
born healthy, in America, with a strong faith, he wasn't
going to let an accident discourage him. "It's much easier to
get back to being who you know you are," he had said just

before I had departed, "than it is to become like someone you don't know."

The following year I got a chance to apply what Larry taught me about faith. Our house on the hill in La Jolla burned down and we lost all of our material possessions. The important thing was that no lives were lost. Even the goldfish and the two turtles, Lightning and Streak, survived.

As the condolences poured in, I began to picture the new structure with a modern kitchen, walk-in closets, and a playroom for the kids. To this day whenever misfortune strikes, I can't seem to find much else to say other than, "No problem, we've had a little, temporary inconvenience." Thank you, Larry.

For over thirty more years, Larry Robb didn't miss a stride. He had several additional tragedies in his life, but he and his wife, Gretta, just continued to move forward. His businesses continued to flourish, his son became a prominent investment executive, and there are plenty of grandkids he nourished with his incurable optimism. When he wasn't fishing, doing deals, hunting, boating on the lake, or playing tennis, he was skiing in Colorado. He gave up inviting me every winter to ski with him.

I'll never forgive myself for not investing several thousand dollars with him forty-something years ago. I'd own a ski resort by now! 🦃

Look at IQ as your
"Imagination Quotient."

Change your attitude and your
lifestyle, and many of your outcomes
will change automatically.

Accept yourself as you are right
now; an imperfect, changing,
growing, and worthy person.

It is not so much what the job gives
you, it's what you give to the job.

You are a masterpiece of creation.

Each human being on earth has equal rights to fulfill his or her own potential.

You are an uncut gemstone of priceless value. Cut and polish your potential with knowledge, skills, and service and you will be in great demand throughout your life.

View stumbling blocks as stepping stones to the stars.

Optimism creates energy and is contagious.

If you believe it, you can achieve it!

Ten Action Steps to Optimism

1. Fly with the eagles. Don't run around with the Henny Pennys who are looking up chanting, "The sky is falling!" Optimism and realism go together. They are the problem-solving twins. Pessimism and cynicism are the two worst companions. Your best friends should be individuals who are the "No problem, it's just a little, temporary inconvenience" type. As you help other people in need on a daily basis, also develop an inner circle of close associations in which the mutual attraction is not sharing problems or needs. The mutual attraction should be values and goals.

2. If you become depressed, visit any one of these four places: a children's hospital, a senior citizen's retirement home, the burn ward at a hospital, or an orphanage. If seeing people worse off than yourself depresses you more, take the positive approach. Take a walk by a playground or park where children are playing and laughing. Catch their spirit of wonder and adventure. Direct your thoughts toward helping others and renewing your faith. Visit your church or synagogue. Sometimes even a change of location can change your thoughts and your feelings.

3. Listen to upbeat, inspiring music. When you are getting ready for work or school, turn on the radio to a good station. Stay away from the morning TV news. You can

brief yourself by scanning the news section on the front page of *The Wall St. Journal* or *New York Times*. It will inform you of all you need to know about the international and national situation affecting your life. Read local news for interest concerning your profession and your family. Resist the temptation to waste time reading the sordid details of someone else's tragedies. Listen to inspirational music or instructional CDs in your car. If possible, have breakfast and lunch with an optimist. Instead of sitting in front of the TV at night, spend time listening to and being involved with those you love.

4. Change your vocabulary. Instead of, "I'm worn out," make it, "I'm relaxed after an active day." Instead of, "Why don't they do something about it?" make it, "I know what I'm going to do." Instead of group griping, try praising someone in the group. Instead of, "Why me, Lord?" make it, "Try me, Lord." Instead of, "The world's a mess," make it, "I'm getting my own house in order."

5. Remember the lobster. At a certain point in a lobster's growth, he discards his outer, protective shell and is vulnerable to all of his enemies. This continues until he grows a new "house" in which to live. Change is normal in life. With every change there is the unfamiliar and the unexpected. Instead of going into a shell, become vulnerable. Risk it! Reach inside for faith in things that are unseen.

6. Get high on your expectations. Instead of, "Relief is just a swallow away," think of, "Belief will help you follow the way." The people you associate with, the places you go, the things you listen to and watch, all are recorded in your thoughts. Since the mind tells the body how to act, think the highest and most uplifting thoughts you can imagine.

7. Engage in positive recreation and education. Select TV programs specializing in the wonders of nature, family health, and cultural enrichment. Select the movies and television you watch for their quality and story value rather than their commercial appeal.

8. Visualize, think, and speak well of your health. Use positive self-talk on a daily basis. Don't dwell on your own small ailments such as colds, headaches, cuts, bruises, muscle pulls, sprains, and minor abrasions. If you pay too much attention to these occurrences they will reward you by becoming your best friends, coming often to pay their respects.

What the mind harbors, the body manifests. This is especially important when you are raising children. Focus on the well family, and dwell on health as the usual environment around your house. I have seen more psychosomatic illnesses in homes where the parents dote on and smother the children with undue concern for their health and safety than in any other type of household. I believe in safety precautions and sound medical practice. I also believe that "your worst" or "your best" concerns will likely come to pass.

9. Call, visit, or write to someone in need, every day of your life. Demonstrate your optimism by passing it on to someone else.

10. Make your day of worship "Good Faith" day. Get into the habit of attending your church, synagogue, mosque, or temple and do some honest listening, and sharing. According to the most recent studies on drug abuse among teenagers and young adults, there are three cornerstones in the lives of those young individuals who do not use drugs of any kind: religious belief, family and extended-family relationships, and high self-esteem.

Going Full Circle
(Tribute to Greg LeMond)

Just when they all cheer you, and when you're at your best
That's when fate steps in to really put you to the test
Just when you feel certain you're going to win it all
Something that you couldn't see causes you to fall

Just when they start thinking
that you'll never win the race
You head right up the mountain
with that look upon your face
And something deep inside you
gives you courage to succeed
And you find the strength to rally in
your darkest hour of need

You've got to bear down when the others all forsake you
You've got to have faith in your heart where it can take you
You go full circle and turn yourself around
Going Full Circle, and make your life rebound
You go full circle and try it once again
Going Full Circle and win!

Chapter Eight

Seeds of Purpose

FOCUS PRECEDES SUCCESS

The Gold Mine in Your Goal Mind

Remember in *Alice in Wonderland* when Alice comes to the junction in the road that leads in different directions and she asks the Cheshire Cat for advice?

"Cheshire-Puss...would you tell me please, which way I ought to go from here?"

"That depends a good deal on where you want to get to," said the Cat.

"I don't much care where..." said Alice.

"Then it doesn't matter which way you go," said the Cat. The grinning feline spoke words of truth, didn't he? If we don't know where we want to go, then any road will take us there—and it doesn't really matter what we do in life.

According to the U.S. Department of Labor, only three out of every one hundred Americans reach age sixty-five with any degree of financial security. Ninety-seven out of one hundred Americans who are sixty-five and over must depend on their monthly Social Security checks to survive. Is this because the Americans dream is shattered? Is it because of constant recessions? All of the world economic conditions have an effect on our personal lives. It is more difficult to survive and thrive during harsh recessions and artificially stimulated recovery cycles, in which the value of our money is eroded. There are, however, internal considerations that I believe are equally as relevant as the environmental circumstances.

Would it surprise you to learn that only five of every one hundred Americans who are in the higher income professions such as law and medicine, reach age sixty-five without having to depend on Social Security? I was astounded to learn that so few individuals achieve any degree of financial success, regardless of their level of income during their most productive years.

Most people live their lives under the delusion that they are immortal. They squander their money, their time, and their minds with activities that are "tension relieving," instead of "goal achieving." Most people work to get through the week with enough extra money to spend over the weekend.

Most people hope that the winds of fate will blow them into some rich and mysterious port of call. They look forward to when they can retire **Someday** in the distant future, and live on a fantasy island **Somewhere**. I ask them how they will accomplish this. They respond **Somehow**.

You have a gold mine in your goal mind. Goals are like gold. Thoughts and dreams are like ore. Until the ore is extracted from the soil, shaped and given form, it has little value.

The reason most people never reach their goals is that they never really set them in the first place. They spend more time planning a vacation than they do planning their own lives. The mind is like the guidance system on a space vehicle or an automatic pilot. Once a goal is set, the mind constantly monitors self-talk and environmental feedback, both positive and negative, making adjustments along the way to reach its target.

Successful individuals have game plans that are clearly defined and to which they constantly refer. They know where they're going every day, every month, and every year. Things don't just happen in their lives. They make life happen for themselves, their organizations, and their loved ones.

Purpose is the engine that powers our lives. If we keep our mind focused on our purpose and the desired result, we can move through routines, details, delays, and around or over any obstacles in our path. Specific, written goals, both for our professional and personal lives, are the tools that make success achievable. Most of us are good at setting professional goals, but often we leave our personal lives to the luck of the draw.

Since the mind is a marvelous bio-computer, it needs specific instructions. Winners know where they are going. And they get there. 🦌

Take Time to Live

Take time to hear a robin's song each morning
Take time to smell the roses as you go
Before you leave, please say "I love you."
To the ones you know
Take time out for a sunset
And its afterglow

Take time to climb a tree with kids this summer
Explore each country back-road you can find
And take a moment now and then
To build a castle in the sand
Take time to hike that mountain
When you can

Take time to play, your work can live without you
Give up the urgent for the afternoon
And take a loved one by the hand
And slowly gaze at that full moon
Don't let this minute pass you
For the years go by too soon

Take the time today
Before it slips away

Take time to live

If you don't know where you're going, it doesn't matter if your alarm doesn't go off in the morning.

Television is technology that lets you watch other people having fun, making money, and achieving their goals.

Your mind is the most marvelous bio-computer ever created. It does not deal with vague ideas; it is activated by specifics.

Most day planners and handheld digital assistants are filled with appointments set by people, other than the owner, to reach their goals.

Written goals are contracts
you make with yourself.

Contentment is for cows. A
challenging purpose is for people.

During the day, ask yourself, "What's
the best use of my time right now?"

Plan the day the day before and
plan the week the week before.

If you go to your place of business to see
what happens, you'll put out fires but
make little progress toward your goals.

What you get is what you set!

Eric the Consummate Goal Setter

In the goal-setting seminars I have been giving through-out the United States and internationally during the past thirty years, it is obvious that the majority of people spend more time planning a party than they do planning their lives. By failing to plan, they actually are planning to fail by default.

In one of my seminars in the midwest many years ago, I divided two hundred participants into groups of six. They sat at circular tables and wrote down and discussed their personal responses to each part in a series of five questions. The questions I asked were these:

1. What are your greatest personal and professional abilities and disabilities?

2. What are your most important personal and professional goals for the balance of the year?

3. What is a major personal and professional goal you have for next year?

4. What will your professional level and annual income be in five years?

5. Twenty years from now:

    Where will you be living?

    What will you be doing?

What will you have accomplished, that could be written or said about you by family or peers?

What state of health will you enjoy?

What will be your assets in money?

After the groaning and grumbling had subsided, the mastermind groups went to work discussing the most important topics they could ever share. As difficult and unreasonable as these questions may appear, you must remember that these two hundred people each paid one-hundred fifty dollars to attend a goal-setting workshop. They seemed dumbfounded that someone actually was challenging them to think about their own lives in specific terms. It was fun to sit and listen to the stories of people crawling out of the ghetto into greatness. But it was no fun to consider doing it yourself. That sounded like being back in school.

As the groups of six got started, I noticed the boy. Eric had red hair, a face full of freckles, and looked about ten. I thought it was a good move for this father to bring him along for some positive exposure on how the adult world operates. He had listened carefully while I had talked, and now he had come up to ask me what the people were doing at the circular tables. I explained that I had given them a series of five questions about their goals in life to discuss in small groups and then asked them to come back later and discuss them with the entire seminar audience.

He mentioned that many of them looked as if they were talking about other things and that some of them were just laughing and telling jokes. I told him that we couldn't expect everyone to take this goal-setting exercise seriously, because many people thought that setting goals was like trying to decide whether to watch TV or go to a movie. He asked me why I wasn't working on my goals at one of the tables. I replied something about being a mentor, and changed the subject by suggesting that it might be fun for him to copy the questions from my notes and try to answer them for his own life. He took one of my yellow-lined pads and a pen and began writing earnestly. When the forty-minute time period was over. I called the small groups back together for the debriefing session.

Question number one had been fairly easy. As I had anticipated, abilities such as "good with people," "sensitive to the needs of others," "dedicated" and "honest" were stated most frequently. Disabilities such as "need to organize time and priorities better" and "want to spend more time on self-improvement projects and more rewarding time with family" also were brought out. These were standard answers from every group.

However, 90 percent of the whole group seemed to find questions two to five difficult—if not impossible—to relate to. Goals for the balance of the year (question two) were "to do better than last year,...to make more, get more, save more, and do more" and "to be a better person." The same kind of general non-committal answers were offered to question three concerning goals for the coming year. The real problems came with questions four and five. When asked what their professional levels and incomes would be in five years they almost all laughed, using the same excuse: "Who can predict in these uncertain times? It depends on the economy." "That' s up to my boss and the company." Most of them did admit, however, that they expected to be at a higher level of employment and earning more money five years from now.

Question five was the real mindblower. In twenty years— where, what doing, what accomplished, how healthy, and what assets? They agonized, giggled, and hollered. One middle-aged man volunteered that he would probably be dead by then. The audience chuckled. Chuckling relieves tension. Most of the group had never considered the question before and came up with inane, nonsensical answers. They said they would be millionaires with yachts anchored off the Isle of Scorpios, or have written famous novels, or have their own TV series. In almost every group the response was the same. No one wanted to forecast or predict his or her own future. They were like all the other groups I had taught, with one exception—the boy named Eric.

When Eric volunteered to come up to the platform and read his answers to the series of five goal-setting questions, the seminar audience was delighted. They looked forward to more laughs and games. I wasn't certain what to expect, but I figured he couldn't be any more wishy-washy than the adults.

"What are your greatest talents and what would you like to improve most, Eric?" I began.

He didn't hesitate. "Building model airplanes and scoring high in video games are my best things and cleaning my bedroom is what I should do better."

I moved on quickly to his personal and professional goals for the rest of the year. He said his personal goal was to complete a model of the Columbia space shuttle craft and that his professional goal was to earn about four hundred and fifty dollars mowing lawns and later shoveling snow. The audience murmured their approval. Now we are getting someplace, I thought to myself.

I asked him what his personal and professional goals were for the coming year. He answered that his personal goal was to take a trip to Hawaii and that his professional goal was to earn seven hundred dollars so that he could pay for the trip. I asked him for more details about the trip. He said it would be during summer vacation, to Honolulu and Maui, on Delta or United—whoever had the best package. I asked him what the hardest part would be in reaching the goal of that trip and he said it would be getting his mom and dad to save enough for their tickets, so that they could take him.

We moved on to Eric's five-year goals. When I asked him about his professional level and income in five years, he still did not hesitate. "I'll be fifteen, and I'll be in the tenth grade in high school," he stated clearly into the microphone. "I plan to take computer courses, if they have any, and science classes. I should be earning two hundred dollars a month, at least, in a part-time job," he stated confidently. The audience wasn't chuckling any more. Even Eric's dad seemed genuinely interested in what the ten-year-old had in mind for this "Fantasy Island" game.

Eric had to think a moment as he considered my question about twenty years from now. He started, "I'll be thirty years old then, right?" I nodded and he continued. "I'll be living in Houston or Cape Canaveral, Florida. I'll be a space-shuttle astronaut working for NASA or a big company. I will have put new TV satellites into orbit and I'll be delivering parts for a new launching station in space. And I'll be in great physical shape. You have to be in good shape to be an astronaut," he concluded proudly.

It was fantastic to hear Eric talk in specifics, whereas all of the adults talked in circles. The impact of what he had said was slowly sinking into the seminar participants. They had paid one hundred fifty dollars each to come and sharpen up their goal-setting skills. A ten-year-old guest had come up and demonstrated how it should be done. The critical difference in Eric was that he hadn't begun to believe that he couldn't achieve his goals. Enough rain had not fallen to ruin his parade. He hadn't watched the evening news enough, or read the paper enough yet. He hadn't taken enough personal defeats. He was unspoiled, naive. His "weakness" of inexperience was his greatest strength.

Eric's thoughtful answers supplied me with one of the best conclusions I have ever had to an all-day seminar. This redheaded kid had accomplished more in ten minutes than I had in five hours of talking. He had taught us that we can talk about our dreams in much more specific, concrete terms if we won't allow our cynicism to stand in our way. Eric had given us all a living example of how goals should be set and pursued.

Eric's perception as a ten-year-old is testimony that the human being is goal-seeking by design. My favorite analogy is one that was taught me by my friend—the late Dr. Maxwell Maltz, plastic surgeon and best-selling author of *Psycho-Cybernetics*. Dr. Maltz compared the mind to the homing system in a torpedo or an automatic pilot. Once you set your target, this self-adjusting system constantly monitors feedback signals from the target area. Using the feedback data to adjust the course setting in its own navigational guidance computer, it makes the correction necessary to stay on target. Programmed incompletely or nonspecifically—or aimed at a target too far out of range— the homing torpedo will wander erratically around until its propulsion system fails or it self-destructs.

The individual human being behaves in very much the same manner. Programmed with vague, random thoughts or fixed on an unrealistic goal too far out of sight, the individual will wander aimlessly around until he gives up in frustration, wears out, or self-destructs.

However, once you set your goal, your mind constantly monitors self-talk and environmental feedback about the goal or target. Using this negative and positive feedback to adjust your decisions along the way, your mind subconsciously makes adjustments to reach the goal.

And what about Eric, the ten-year-old who attended one of my goal setting seminars more than forty years ago? One morning, years ago, I was shaving and watching *The Today Show* reflected in the mirror of my bathroom. A NASA astronaut was outside the space shuttle retrieving a satellite that had to be brought back to earth for repairs. I nearly cut myself with my razor, when I recognized the grown-up version of Eric, the red-haired kid, minus the freckles.

It was actually him! He had achieved his twenty-year fantasy of becoming an astronaut, and I hadn't given it another thought since I wrote about Eric in one of my books. As I wiped the shaving cream off my face, I took a good look at myself in the mirror and asked myself a question: While young Eric had been focused on his dreams during the past twenty years, had I been true to my own? Was I practicing what I was preaching? Was I so busy teaching other people how to set and get their goals, that I was putting my own on layaway?

The young boy from one of my seminars—turned astronaut—gave me a needed wake-up call. It's one thing to talk and write about goals, and another thing entirely to stay focused on reaching your own. 🐦

There is a gold mine, in your goal mind!

What you can clearly visualize,
you can realize.

If you don't set goals, your mind will
set one to get through the day.

With focused, concentrated goals you
have the power of a laser beam.

Ask yourself: "If there were no
constraints of money, time, or
circumstance, what would I
begin doing tomorrow?"

The reason most people don't reach their goals, is that they never really set them in the first place.

Most people spend more time planning a vacation or a party than they spend planning their lives.

Purpose is the engine that powers our lives.

Focus always precedes success.

There is no such thing as a time management problem, only focus problems that steal time from priorities.

My Daughter and Her Doggone Goal

Not long after young Eric—the astronaut-to-be—attended my goal-setting seminar in Iowa, I took one of my daughters, Dayna, to another goal workshop in San Diego. She was unusually quiet as we drove home. She had something brewing in that pretty little head.

Several days later I noticed strange occurrences around our household. I stubbed my toe on what appeared to be a heavy metal Frisbee lying hollow side up in the kitchen. "Who put this landmine in front of my refrigerator?" I howled at my kids, who were eating Count Chockula cereal with sliced bananas on it. Dayna answered brightly, "I did, Dad. That's my dog's dish."

"How can that be your dog's dish when we don't have a dog?" I retorted, knowing this was some kind of trick (we have a history of ingenious practical jokes that we perpetrate on each other to keep the family alert).

"He's my imaginary dog, Dad. But he's becoming so real that I had to buy his dish this week, so we can feed him when he gets here!" she blurted excitedly. "Let me pour cold water on this dog-goal of yours in a hurry," I scolded, swallowing a spoonful of bananas and cereal. "That dish is big enough for a horse and, besides, we're not getting a dog right now, full stop!"

She came right back at me, "But you said if you really set your mind on something and get all the information on it then..." I interrupted her as parents normally do. "I know what I said," I answered, "but that was at the seminar, and we're at home now. Children can't set their own goals without the prior consent of the great goalkeeper, and that's me!" The children ate their cereal in silence, packed their lunches, kissed me good-bye, and went to school.

When I came home from a meeting that Saturday afternoon, I saw Dayna walking around the yard talking to a long chain that she was dragging behind her in one hand. I interrogated her as soon as I walked out of the garage. "What are you doing talking to yourself with that piece of chain in your hand?" I inquired. "It's not a piece of chain, Dad," she corrected me. "It's my dog's leash and I'm practicing taking him for a walk." I told her to practice in her room because the neighbors might be watching and they thought we were a bit strange already.

I knew I'd been a little gruff with my kids on the dog issue, so I decided to smooth things over and humor my daughter a little by appearing to be interested in her goal. "If you should get a dog, at some future date when we move, what kind of dog would you get, honey," I inquired softly. "Yorkie or poodle?"

You know I don't like little lapdogs, Dad," she sighed. "My dog's a malamute." My recollection of malamutes was that they are large dogs, with huge appetites, and that they are designed to pull sleds in the Arctic. I reminded her that we lived in Southern California where it was balmy all year, and that the poor dog would pant and shed its fur, seeking shelter under a tree all summer long. "And besides," I added, "he probably would smell."

She had a one-track, monorail mind. "You're right, Dad," she replied, "malamutes have great noses. He'll always find his way back home and he'll be a great watchdog, you'll see."

The situation was getting desperate, but I knew I held the "ace cards" in the form of the checkbook and the absolute veto power when I was outvoted in family council meetings. "If you were to get this dog, which you won't for a year or so, do you know approximately what he would look like?" I asked Dayna after dinner. Her answer caught me a little off guard.

"He's got a black fur coat, with brown on his tummy and upper legs," she said admiringly. "He has a white diamond on his forehead and beautiful brown eyes," she beamed. She pulled out a little pocketbook entitled *The Care and Feeding of Malamutes* and flipped through the pages. "You'll learn to love Kheemo, Dad," she said confidently, reminding me of myself when I tried to convince the children that broccoli and cauliflower were delicious.

"What do you mean, Kheemo?" I asked, trying to control the irritation I was beginning to feel with this impossible "wishful thinking."

"Kheemo is his name, Dad," she sighed, "it's an abbreviation for the name Kheemosabe (Kheemo-sah-beh), which is an Indian expression meaning 'good friend.' "I reminded her that I grew up listening to the Lone Ranger every week on the radio and that I was well aware of the expression that Tonto used to greet his friend, the masked man. Feeling that we had reached an impasse in the discussion, I broke off the dog debate and we went into the living room to join the other members of the family.

The next day was Father's Day. I should have realized it was going to be a special day all right. I had been set up by my own children for the payoff on the very day they were supposed to honor me.

I came down the stairs that Sunday morning determined to spend the kind of Father's Day I had always dreamed of. I came to the breakfast table in my pajamas, bathrobe, and slippers, with the *TV Guide* in one hand and the morning paper in the other. "Today, we're going to the second service at church and afterwards, I'm going to concentrate on doing absolutely nothing," I announced to the family. "I'm going to sit around in my bathrobe, relax, and watch baseball and old movies all day," I added, with a touch of arrogance. I noticed that the kids were all dressed, with their hair combed and their jackets on, as if they were going on an outing. I opened my Father's Day card and taped at the bottom, after all the endearing poetry, was a classified ad from the morning paper.

Last of the litter. One adorable AKC male malamute puppy. Pure-bred, papers, shots. Only $500. Drive by today. This one won't last. Ideal children's pet.

"Don't you want to take your children for a drive after church on Father's Day?" the little darlings chimed in together.

"As a matter of fact, that's exactly what I don't want to do," I retorted, sticking my nose in the *TV Guide* to see what time the game came on. Their response, obviously well rehearsed, sounded like something out of Harry Chapin's classic song "The Cat's in the Cradle."

"That's OK, Dad, don't be blue, 'cause we're gonna grow up just like you,'" they chanted. "Someday when you're old and gray, you'll want us to visit you on Father's Day," they continued. "You'll say, 'Come over kids and visit me,' but we'll say, 'Sorry, Dad, we're watchin' TV.' Oh, that's OK, Dad, don't be blue, 'cause we're gonna grow up just like you.'"

On our way over to the kennels after church, I lectured the children on the absolute rules of conduct for the rest of the day. They were to go up and play with the malamute puppy for a few minutes and I would stay in the car, listening to the baseball game. They would get all the information on the dog and we would then go home better informed, in case we ever got serious about owning a dog. I brought out all the reasons why we weren't going to get the dog, I started with the responsibilities, the problem of caring for it when we were away from home, the possibility of rabies, the risk of it biting the mailman and our being sued. And I finished with all of the important issues a prudent family must consider, before making such a costly investment.

At the kennels I couldn't understand what was taking them so long to get the information on the puppy. Surely the kennel owners had better things to do than let a gang of children play with their merchandise for half an hour. As I opened the car door to go up and see what was keeping the children, a furry ball with four legs came scrambling toward me. He was black with a brown tummy and there was a white diamond on his forehead, between two, big brown eyes. I think it was the eyes that did it. He licked my shoes and pulled at my trousers. He ran around me in circles with his little curved tail wagging so furiously that he looked like an anchored-down helicopter trying to take off. He lay on his back, looking up at me, inviting me to scratch his chest and stomach. He knew who his master was! I said, "Get in the car, Kheemo; let's go home and watch the ball game."

The dog cost five hundred dollars. The fence cost five hundred dollars. He ate the webbing off the patio furniture. He destroyed the flower garden. He chewed up my house slippers and my best jogging shoes. He came right in the house through the porch screen door, which was locked.

Shortly after his arrival, the kids and I were roughhousing with him in the family room, while my wife was out shopping. Unfortunately, we had selected my wife's favorite Persian rug to romp on and the situation soon got out of hand. As Kheemo and I were doing battle, the dog attacked the rug and sent the fibers flying in all directions.

My wife's Persian masterpiece had a winter scene woven intricately out of different colored threads and textured yarns. In the center was a Canadian snow goose taking flight from a tranquil pond. Evidently malamutes are near-sighted because Kheemo was eating the goose as if it were a gourmet dinner. I grabbed the puppy's jaws and managed to retrieve most of the loose threads before he swallowed them. For the next two hours I tried to weave the loose strings back through the warp and weft threads in the rug in some pattern that would resemble a Canadian snow goose. What I ended up with looked more like a wet turkey!

When my wife returned from the store, the children and I were in the process of straightening the rug and putting our weaving tools away. "What happened to my rug?" she exclaimed, coming closer to examine it. I waved her away. "It's nothing to worry about," I said casually; "the kids and I were chasing around the yard and the house, and we got your Persian rug a little soiled. We shampooed it for you and it would be better for you not to walk on it just yet. Why don't you want until tomorrow to check it over, after it dries?" I suggested nervously. "It doesn't look right," she said, shaking her head. Before I could stop her she grabbed the vacuum cleaner and sucked the center right out of the rug, where the snow goose had been. "Good heavens," she shrieked, "what have you done to my priceless rug?" I made the weak excuse that it must have been one of those counterfeited Iranian rugs that don't hold up under normal environmental conditions.

"It was your dog that did this, wasn't it?" my wife said, her voice wavering with emotion. "It wasn't my dog," I argued apologetically, "it was our daughter Dayna's dog that chewed up the rug." "You bought it" my wife answered coldly. "But she thought it," I countered, proclaiming my innocence.

The temperature was rather frigid around the house for the next week or two. Every time my wife walked past the spot where the rug used to lie she muttered things about dogs and husbands as if they belonged together. She also said she wished lecturers would practice what they preached at seminars.

As for Kheemo, he grew up to be a fine family pet and watchdog. Dayna and the rest of the kids grew up to believe in their dreams. And they realize how important it is to be very specific about what you want and to consider how achieving your goals will impact the people around you. 🐾

Chapter Nine

Seeds of Family Leadership

EMPOWERING OTHERS

Children Learn
What They Live

An ancient Chinese proverb tells us, "A child's life is like a piece of paper on which every passerby leaves a mark." We cannot teach our children self-esteem. We can only help them discover it within themselves by adding positive marks and strokes on their slates.

All positive motivation is rooted in self-esteem—the development of which, just as with other skills, takes practice. Think of self-esteem as a four-legged chair.

A Sense of Belonging

The first leg of self-esteem is a sense of belonging. We all have a deep-seated need to feel we're part of something larger than ourselves. This need, which psychologists call an affiliation drive, encompasses people, places, and possessions. Our instinct for belonging—for being wanted, accepted, enjoyed, and loved by close ones—is extremely powerful. It explains the bond of an extended family, friends, and teammates. It also explains why some adolescents join gangs. They want to belong, even if it's wrong.

Make your children proud of their family heritage and make your home a place where they feel safe, loved, and welcome. Also, make your home a place where your children want to bring their friends, rather than a place they want to leave as soon as possible.

A Sense of Individual Identity

The second leg, which complements the sense of belonging, is a sense of individual identity. No human being is exactly like another, not even an identical twin. We are all unique combinations of talents and traits that never existed before and will never exist again in quite the same package. (This explains why most parents believe their children came from different planets!)

Observe your children as they grow and play. Watch their learning styles. Notice what they love to do in their free time. Help them discover their unique positive talents and help nurture them into skills. Report cards don't necessarily measure talents. They often are a measure only of discipline, memory, and attention span.

A Sense of Worthiness

The third leg of self-esteem is a sense of worthiness, the feeling that I'm glad I'm me, with my genes and background, my body, my unique thoughts. Without our own approval, we have little to offer. If we don't feel worth loving, it's hard to believe that others love us; instead, we tend to see others as appraisers or judges of our value.

Show your children unconditional love. Carefully separate the doer from the deed, and the performer from the performance.

The message: "I love you no matter what happens, and I'm always there for you" is one of the most important concepts in building a feeling of worthiness or intrinsic value in children. After every reprimand, let them know you love them. Before they go to sleep at night, give them the reassurance that, regardless of what happened that day, you love them unconditionally.

A healthy sense of belonging, identity, and worthiness can only be rooted in intrinsic core values as opposed to outer, often material, motivation. Without them, we depend on others constantly to fill our leaking reserves of self-esteem—but also tend to suspect others of ulterior motives. Unable to accept or reject others' opinions for what they're worth, we are defensive about criticism and paranoid about praise—and no amount of praise can replace the missing qualities.

A healthy sense of belonging, identity, and worthiness is also essential to belief in your dreams. It is most essential during difficult times, when you have only a dream to hang on to.

A Sense of Control and Competence

Early in my career in motivational psychology, I thought the chair of self-esteem balanced firmly on those three legs, especially since they involved intrinsic core values.

It took much time and research to realize that a fourth leg—one of the most important—was missing.

There are many reasons why few Americans currently in high school and college believe they were born to win. The supportive extended family—in many cases, even the nuclear family—is disappearing. Role models are increasingly unhealthy. The commercial media bombards young senses ever more insistently with crime, violence, hedonism, and other unhealthy forms of escape. But whatever the explanation, constructive citizens and leaders in society cannot emerge and develop without the creative imagination that serves them like fuel—which is why the apprehension, frustration, and hesitation I see and hear in the younger generation is cause for concern. At the moment, the future they imagine will help drive neither happiness nor success.

The chair's fourth leg is self-efficacy, a functional belief in your ability to control what happens to you in a changing, uncertain world. A sense of worthiness may give you the emotional means to venture, but you need self-efficacy, the sense of competence and control, to believe you can succeed. That's why it is so important to assign responsibility for small tasks to your children as early as possible so they can learn that their choices and efforts result in consequences and successes. The more success they experience, the stronger their confidence grows—and the more responsibility they want to assume.

Give them specific household chores and duties they can accomplish and be proud of. Teach them that their problems and setbacks are just temporary inconveniences and learning experiences. Emphasize it constantly: Setbacks are not failures.

Armed with a view of failure as a learning experience, children can develop an early eagerness for new challenges and will be less afraid to try new skills. Although they appreciate compliments, they benefit most from their own belief that they are making a valuable contribution to life, according to their own internal standards.

In an increasingly competitive global marketplace, each new, young member of the workforce simply must believe that he or she is a team leader, a self-empowered, quality individual who expresses that quality in excellent production and service. With increasing pressures on profit and the need to do more with fewer workers because of e-commerce and changing technology, it is essential that parents and business leaders help raise the value of their childrens' and employees' stock in themselves.

Our Kids Are Not Our Clones

One of the most valuable lessons I have learned in being an effective family leader and in raising six children is to: "Treat our children with the same respect, we expect from them."

Our children are not clones or copies of us. Although they mimic us and other adults as role models, they cannot be expected to feel or act the way we do. Kahlil Gibran is my favorite on the subject:

Your children are not your children.

They are the sons and daughters
of Life's longing for itself...

You may give them your love
but not your thoughts,

For they have their own thoughts.

You may house their bodies but not their souls,

For their souls dwell in the house of
tomorrow, which you cannot visit,

Not even in your dreams.

You may strive to be like them, but
seek not to make them be like you.

For life goes not backward nor
tarries with yesterday[5] ✿

---

5. Gilbran, Kahlil, *The Prophet* (New York: Alfred A. Knopf, 1972), p. 17

Take a Moment

Take a moment to listen today to what
your children are trying to say,
Listen to them, whatever you do or
they won't be there to listen to you.

Listen to their problems,
listen to their needs
Praise their smallest triumphs,
praise their littlest deeds;
Tolerate their chatter,
amplify their laughter,
Find out what's the matter,
find out what they're after.

If we tell our children all
the bad in them we see,
They'll grow up exactly how we
hoped they'd never be;
But if we tell our children
we're so proud to wear their name,
They'll grow up believing that
they're winners in the game.

So tell them that you love them
every single night;
And though you scold them
make sure you hold them
and tell them they're all right,
"Good night, happy dreams,
Tomorrow's looking bright."

Take a moment to listen today to what
your children are trying to say
Listen to them whatever you do, and
they'll be there to listen to you.

The world needs role models,
instead of critics.

Others know when you have
their best interests at heart.

Come through for others, and they
will come through for you.

If everyone is thinking alike,
then someone isn't thinking.

Success is doing your own thing,
for the benefit of others.

A true friend is someone you can trust.

People who seek attention, need
all the help they can get.

Real power comes by empowering others!

The only people you will influence
to any great degree will be the
people you care about.

Your best friend should bring
out the best in you.

Where Are My Children?

Have you seen anywhere, a dear boy and a girl,
and their small winsome brother of four?

It was only today that barefoot and brown,
they played by my kitchen door;

It was only today, or maybe a year,
it couldn't be twenty I know,

That laughing and singing they called me to
play, but I was too busy to go. Too busy with
my work and my life to play; and now they've
grown up and they've wandered away.

Someday, I know, they must stop and look back, and
wish they were children again. And, Oh, just to hold
them, and hug them again, I'd run out my kitchen door.

For there's never a chore, that could keep me away,
could I just hear my children call me to play;

Where are my children? I've got time—today! [6]

---

6. Written by the author's mother, Irene Waitley, 1944

Promises should not be given lightly
unless you want them lightly received.

You know you're a success
when people tell you, "I like me
best when I'm with you."

No one cares how much you know
about achieving your dreams, until
they know how much you care about
helping them achieve their own dreams.

You are truly successful when you can extend a strong hand to someone who is reaching out or just trying to hang on.

If we succeed without sacrifice, it's because someone sacrificed for us.

Here are some tips for healthy personal relationships and raising win-win children:

1. Look at yourself through others' eyes. Imagine being married to you. Imagine being your child or your friend.

2. Check to see if you shift roles easily and appropriately from worker/executive and earner to nurturing parent, and from role model to romantic partner.

3. Be empathic in your communications. Knowledge isn't always wisdom, sensitivity isn't always accuracy, sympathy isn't always understanding. Really get inside another person before you pass judgment or offer advice. Ask questions, listen, and discover rather than making assumptions.

4. Listen unconditionally to the significant adults and children in your life. Listening without bias or distraction is the greatest value you can pay another person.

5. Develop a magic touch. Don't assume that money, shelter, and creature comforts are enough to demonstrate your love. Nothing can replace your presence, your hug, your touch—you.

6. Be aware of opportunities to add spice and romance to your most important adult relationship: flowers, a greeting card slipped into a briefcase, an unexpected

phone call, an overnight bag in the car trunk when it was supposed to be just dinner and a movie.

7. Talk casually and evenly with your children, not as an authority figure. Parents under stress often withdraw from one another and from their children, communicating in a terse, irritated way. To ensure that your children feel accepted, take time to chat with them about anything and everything, a message that says "I'm interested in you."

8. Become enthusiastic about your family members' interests. Young children need their parents' involvement and approval—but remember that involvement shouldn't mean taking over or becoming their agent and manager.

9. Schedule mandatory family time together, even at the expense of seemingly pressing obligations. Family members often meet coming and going, making the home like a pit stop at the Indianapolis 500. One meal a day together with the television off is a bare minimum.

10. Build a home atmosphere in which each family member respects the needs, dignity, and individuality of all the others. Make your cornerstones love, caring, trust, and giving.

11. Maintain an atmosphere that encourages free and open communications. Encourage all family members

to express feelings and opinions without fear of recrimination or reprisal. ॐ

Roots and Wings
(A Child's Bedtime Song)

If I had two wishes, I know what they would be
I'd wish for roots to cling to, and wings to set me free;
Roots of inner values, like rings within a tree
And wings of independence to seek my destiny.

Roots to hold forever to keep me safe and strong
To let me know you love me,
when I've done something wrong;
To show me by example, and help me learn to choose
To take those actions every day to win instead of lose.

Just be there when I need you, to tell me it's all right
To face my fear of falling when I test my wings in flight;
Don't make my life too easy, it's better if I try
And fail and get back up myself, so I can learn to fly.

If I had two wishes, and two were all I had
And they could just be granted, by my mom and dad;
I wouldn't ask for money or any store-bought things
The greatest gifts I'd ask for are simply roots and wings.

Chapter Ten

Seeds of Motivation

WINNING FROM WITHIN

The Inner Winner

You may recall from history that the exquisitely beautiful, armless statue of Venus de Milo was carved by an unknown sculptor.

When a farmer dug up the soon-to-be world-famous work of art while plowing his field, a renowned museum official sadly reflected what a great pity it was that the sculptor would never be recognized by thousands of admirers, nor would he ever know how valuable the statue became hundreds of years later.

The farmer retorted that it must have been a labor of love for someone to be able to have envisioned such perfection and bring it forth with just a chisel and a shapeless piece of stone. "Just creating something of such quality," said the farmer, "would have been payment in full for me."

You can't commission a masterpiece. Human greatness can't be externally motivated. It must be compelled from within.

Do you see what that means for you? If you want to be the best—whether it's the best manager, the best salesperson, the best parent, or the best athlete in a sport—you have to light that fire within yourself. Real motivation is that drive from within. You know where you're going because you have a compelling image inside, not a travel poster on the wall.

This is why the words empower and envision are so vital to team performance and quality. It must be their power and vision that compels them, not that of their leader.

The success of our efforts depends not so much on the efforts themselves, but rather on our motive for doing them. The greatest companies and the greatest men and women in all walks of life have achieved their greatness out of a desire to express something within themselves that had to be expressed, a desire to solve a problem using their skills as best they could.

This is not to say that many of these individuals did not earn a great deal of money and prestige for what they produced. Many did. But the key to their successes is to be found in the fact that they were motivated more by providing excellence in a product or service to fill a need than by any thought of profit. William Shakespeare, Thomas Edison, Estee Lauder, Oprah Winfrey, Bill Gates, and Michael Dell all became wealthy. Separated as they are in time and type of talent, they were all motivated by the same thing: to produce the very best, to express the very best that was in them.

Dr. Martin Luther King, Jr. spoke about this as eloquently as anyone ever has when he said, "If an individual is called to be a streetsweeper, he or she should sweep streets even as Michelangelo painted, or Beethoven composed music, or Shakespeare wrote poetry. He should sweep streets so well, that all the hosts of Heaven and Earth will pause and say, here lived a great streetsweeper who did his job well."

We would be well to read the biography of Colin Powell, former Chairman of the Joint Chiefs of Staff, and Secretary of State of the United States. Growing up, he was said to have been one of the best streetsweepers in his urban neighborhood. 🦅

Motivation is an inner force that compels behavior. Your inner drives will propel you further and faster than external perks.

Without a sense of urgency, desire loses its value.

It's difficult to be depressed and active at the same time. When you're feeling blue, stop thinking about "you" and go out and help someone with even greater needs.

You always move in the direction of your current dominant thoughts.

We can change if we want to.

You can't concentrate on the reverse of an idea. A fear is a goal moving in the opposite direction from your desire.

Put up the dream. Put in the knowledge. Put out the effort.

Think of your imagination as a skill rather than a talent and learn to use it.

Motivation is motive in action.

The two greatest fear busters are knowledge and action.

Winning Is

Winning is never whining.

*Winning is coming in fourth, exhausted but
excited, because you came in fifth last time.*

*Winning is treating animals like people
and people like brothers and sisters.*

Winning is being glad you're you.

Winning is a feeling, there is no ceiling.

*Winning is beginning, and by beginning,
the game is half won.*

Winning is all in the attitude!

How to Find the Olympian Within

You're standing on the highest pedestal, the one in the center. You hear the roar of approval from the crowd. As the first note of the national anthem is played in the Olympic stadium, you feel all the pride and honor that accompanies this moment.

Ten thousand hours of preparation for this one triumphant moment in history. You've won the gold!

That dream of an Olympic championship is in the heart of every amateur athlete, just as the Grand Final, World Cup, Super Bowl, and Wimbledon are the goals of professional football players and tennis players. What are your dreams? You're most likely not a world-class athlete, but surely you have aspirations of your own. Perhaps you imagine a metaphorical gold medal being placed around your neck by the CEO of your company, or by your friends and family for being the best in your own unique way. Maybe you wonder whether you're up to the risk of starting your own business.

On Sundays my grandparents would take us children to ride the huge merry-go-round next to the San Diego Zoo. We could hardly wait to mount those bobbing zebras, lions, tigers, and stallions, and whirl round and round to the music of the antique pipe organ. Surrounded by mirrors and lights, our hearts would pound in anticipation as we stretched out desperately, trying to be the one among all the riders who would grab the gold ring and win another ride. So began my competitive spirit.

Since you're probably younger than I am, you may never even have heard of grabbing the gold ring on the carousel. But in the 1940s and 50s, if you reached out and caught it, you not only got a free ride—your name was also announced over the loudspeaker and all the other kids and their parents would applaud. And, of course, the kids all wished it could have been them instead of you.

Reflecting back now on my youth, I've come to some realizations. I guess I did start out thinking of success and winning as something that you got by reaching outside yourself and proving to others that you were worthy. Come to think of it, most of my friends also believed that you had to prove, or earn, or win, or perform in some special way, and then you would deserve the gold ring or the Olympic gold medal.

The approval of others seemed to precede feelings of self-confidence and self-worth. You were entitled to feel good about yourself only after you performed well. Why did it take me so many years to discover that just the reverse ought to be true?

After devoting most of my lifetime to investigating the well-springs of personal and professional success, I'm able to make the following statements with great confidence:

You need to feel love inside yourself before you can offer it to anyone else. Your own sense of value determines the quality of your performance. Performance is only a reflection of internal worth, not a measure of it. The less you try to impress, the more impressive you are. What you show the world on the outside is a mirror image of how you feel on the inside.

You should chase your passion, not your pension.

The key trait shared by athletic champions and winners in every walk of life is the fundamental belief in one's own internal value.

If your success depends on external possessions, you'll be subject to constant anxiety. When your peer group cheers one of your accomplishments, you'll feel good for a while, but then you'll wonder if they'll cheer as loudly the next time. If they're critical, you will feel hurt and threatened. The truth is, you can never win over a long period of time if your concept of success depends upon the perfect performance or the placing of a gold medal around your neck.

It's obvious that talent, looks, and other attributes aren't equally distributed, but we're all given an abundance of value—more than we could use in several lifetimes. The game of life certainly isn't played on a level playing field for each of us in terms of education, a supportive home life, and other circumstances beyond our control, but I can assure you that you were born with the qualities of a champion. That's what I mean by value.

You see, champions are born, but they can be unmade by their perceptions, exposure, and responses. Losers are not born to lose. They're programmed that way by their own responses to their environment and their decisions.

There's a phrase I like to use—The Inner Winner—that describes the kind of person who recognizes his or her internal value, and who is able to use that recognition as the foundation for achieving any goal. The secret of wearing the gold medal around your neck in the external world is that first you must be an Inner Winner. You must recognize that you're already an Olympian Within. 🐎

Words to Forget	*Words to Remember*
I can't	**I can**
I'll try	**I will**
I have to	**I choose to**
Should have	**Will do**
If only	**Next time**
Problem	**Opportunity**
Difficult	**Challenging**
Stressed	**Motivated**
I, me, my	**You, your**
Yes, but	**Yes, let's do it**
Hate	**Love**

Dream big and believe you
are worthy of success.

Losers say "It's not my fault!" Winners
say: "Here's how we're going to fix it."

Losers let it happen. Winners
make it happen.

Good time management means you
maximize the daily return on the
energy and mental effort you expend.

Giant oaks do grow from little acorns;
but first you must have an acorn!

The only secret to success is that
you have to go out and do.

It's not the experience of today that
causes us the most stress, it's the regret
for something we didn't do yesterday.

LUCK is an acronym, Laboring
Under Correct Knowledge.

Think of motivation as steam. If released
into the open air it vanishes. But if
harnessed and focused it catapults
jet airplanes off aircraft carriers.

You are what you do.

Give your best effort, because you
are worth your best effort.

Don't put success and happiness
on layaway. Do it now!

Winners take time to look at the
rosebuds opening each day.

Winners take time to listen—knowing
there may be fewer robins next spring.

Winners take time for children—too
soon they fly like arrows from the bow.

They take time to play—knowing that
when children grow up they get old.

Winners take time for old people—
knowing that old people live for
the next visit from a loved one.

They take time for nature—knowing
they can't put it on their Mastercard.

Winners take time for their health—
knowing it's the single gift you're
given, that you don't recognize and
appreciate until it leaves you.

They take time to read—knowing that books are the fountains of wisdom that take you where you can't always go in person and offer you what you don't need to learn by your own mistakes.

Winners take time to work—knowing they can't enjoy the view unless they scale the mountain.

Life is a marvelous game of choice, not chance; with no time outs, no substitutions, and the clock is always running. It is not a scrimmage, or a drill, and there are no instant replays. Every day is the Superbowl!

Losers see thunderstorms.
Winners see rainbows.

Losers worry about the icy streets.
Winners put on their ice skates.

Losers are aggressive and take all
they can get. Winners are assertive,
getting what they want by helping
others get what they need.

Chapter Eleven

Seeds of Communication

ASK AND LISTEN

Can You Hear Me Now?
Listening and Leadership

Even the most enlightened conception of leadership can't work without constructive communication—but how to achieve that?

Not by technique alone. We must constantly ask ourselves if we are operating with the old win-lose approach of position power rather than the new win-win approach of relationship power. Is our interest in others only for what they can do for us? Are we in this or that relationship primarily to satisfy our needs? Do we give as little as possible in return for a reward we envision?

The best communication techniques in the world won't fool most people for very long. Still, if your understanding of the substance of relationships is solid, learning new techniques for management communications can make a very significant difference. Empowered teams require a new communication style. In a traditional work group, you want compliance. In an empowered team, you want initiative. Directional communication (announcing decisions, issuing orders) inhibits team input. If the team leader or supervisor is still using "boss" language, the team gets the message that they're being told what to do. Managers of empowered teams need to learn to ask open-ended questions and develop the skill of truly listening to the answers.

Listening is a lost art, which must be rediscovered. Few people really listen to others, usually because they're too busy thinking about what they want to say next. In business transactions, clear communication is often colored by power plays, one-upmanship, and attempts to impress rather than to express. In our work, as well as our personal lives, how we listen is at least as important as how we talk. Genuine listening to what others want would allow more sales to be made, more deals to be closed and greater productivity to be gained. Although it's not always necessary or possible to satisfy those wants, understanding them is the glue of a relationship.

Not paying value by listening is a way of saying, "You're not important to me." The results are reduced productivity (I don't count here, so why should I even try?), employee turnover (Who wants to work in a place where I don't feel valued?), absenteeism (I'm just a cog in the wheel, only noticed when I make a mistake), retaliation (They only listen when the griping gets loud enough), lost sales (They don't seem to understand what I need), and dangling deals (I can't get through to them; it's like talking to a brick wall). Genuine listening can cure a remarkable range of supposedly intractable problems.

Even if you have excellent presentation skills and have an authoritative and persuasive ability to speak to those you lead, make a conscious effort to convert your team meetings into creative dialogue where you ask open-ended questions and solicit feedback and input from all those present. Everyone can be a source of useful ideas. The people closest to the problem usually have the best ideas. Learning flows up as well as down in the organization. Nothing is sacred except the governing vision and values. The process of open dialogue improves performance. The more information people can access, the better.

Most importantly, don't view any suggestion or comment from the group as inane, silly, or irrelevant. Appearing foolish in front of one's peers is a major embarrassment and stifles any future desires to offer ideas that might be considered "off the wall." The most common mistake in communicating is saying what you want to say, rather than what they need to hear and then listening to what they have to offer. It's rightly been said that you can get more people to vote for you in twenty minutes by showing interest in them, than you can in twenty weeks by showing how interesting you are. 🌱

Living Is Giving

Living is giving your best self away,
Living is helping someone every day;
Living is giving more than you get,
It's treating an animal like a person, instead of a pet.

It's helping the handicapped across the street,
It's smiling at the new person at work that you meet;
It's respect for all nations, color and creeds,
It's sharing and caring for your neighbor's needs

Losers keep betting that living is "getting"
But there's one of God's laws that they keep on forgetting
And this is the one you can live and believe
The more that you give, the more you'll receive!

If you must speak, ask a question.

Unless what you say benefits the other person, don't say it.

When you talk you learn nothing.

It's not what I think that counts, nor is it what you think that counts. It's what I think you think and what you think I think, that really counts.

Perception is reality in the eyes of the beholder.

If you attack another person's beliefs,
you are creating an enemy.

Learn to express, not impress.

No one listens to a person operating
out of self-interest alone.

Sin has many tools, but a lie is
the handle that fits them all.

Your word is more
valuable than money.

Why Bad News Sells

My favorite news commentator is the venerable Paul Harvey, with whom I've been privileged to share many platforms. Paul has observed on many occasions that much of the modern media features bad guys who seem to win. The well-behaved, healthy, and happily married won't be showcased on television, he comments, because they tend to make watchers subconsciously feel sorry for themselves. The tabloid readership is intrigued by a successful person only when he or she is involved in a scandal, stricken with an illness, commits a crime, or loses a fortune. Every hospital always has patients worse off to make us feel comparably fortunate.

Harvey calls this the "we're glad we weren't the victim of the day" syndrome. The plane crash we weren't in, the beautiful actress who had a mastectomy, the star athlete fallen from his pedestal, the public official in trouble—such stories will dominate the headlines as long as the fire that burns them warms the rest of us. But Harvey sounds an even more compelling warning about the effects of bad news. He believes it tends to sour us on a way of life that is the envy of the rest of the world. Much social rebellion, he suggests, may be a reflection of cynicism caused by the media's exaggerated focus on what's wrong rather than what we could be doing right. We're inculcating the opposite of leadership. The younger generation is receiving a model for losing rather than for winning.

"Americans aren't so ugly, so cruel, so corrupt, so licentious as the headlines imply," Harvey says. He quoted a Princeton Research Survey of two thousand heads of households—revealing that American family values are alive and doing fairly well. Ninety percent of those polled do not steal, 86 percent are married, 84 percent don't cheat on their spouses, 88 percent don't spread lies about others. When we hear that almost 50 percent of American marriages end in divorce, we should know that the high percentage of repeaters leads to misinterpretation of that number. Clearly, the sensationalist obsession on the small aberrational segment of our population is being forced on the rest of us—who live relatively mundane lives, trying to be successful and to maintain a positive attitude.

The next time you sit down for a dose of "Reality TV," be aware that you are watching the lifestyles of one of the smallest segments of our population. The more outrageous and raunchy the content, the higher the ratings. Why? Entertainment producers know that "shock value" sells tickets and attracts lookers like a horrific highway traffic accident. Bad news may sell, but it doesn't inspire authentic leadership.

Take the high road by setting an example in your own life worthy of emulating by those who look to you as a role model, mentor, and coach. Be a good news anchor! ❧

Few of us have enough virtue
to resist the highest bidder.

It is better to earn the trust and respect
of one of your children, than to gain
notoriety and adulation of the masses.

Moderation in temper is always a virtue.
Moderation in principle is always a vice.

The greatest destroyer of self-esteem is to
be criticized in public or in front of peers.

Emperors are overthrown.
Empowerers are revered.

Before you state your case, gather
the evidence, especially what
motivates the other person.

Marriage is not total agreement. It is
looking in the same direction together.

When you communicate think: "I'll
make you glad you talked to me today!"

When you communicate hope the
other person is thinking: "I like
me best when I'm with you."

The Woman in the Mirror

Mirror, Mirror on my wall,
What's the meaning of it all?
Is there something more to life,
Than to be a loving wife?

Yes, I'll love my children dearly,
But they'll grow up and come by yearly.
Dare I yearn to know myself and the
talents hidden on the shelf?

What about the needs I feel?
Are my dreams considered real?
I want to learn, I want to teach
I want to earn, I want to reach
I want to fly from my cocoon and
Put my footsteps on the moon.

I'm not angry or rebelling, but there's
something strong, compelling.
I don't want to be a man,
I love the woman that I am.
I can give the world so much
With my special female touch. .

Mirror, Mirror on my wall
Help me help him hear my call.
All I ever hope to be is
Free—to be that person, Me!

Man Gazing into Future

Crystal ball, oh crystal ball
Will my empire rise and fall
Like the Roman legions must
Ash to ash, and dust to dust?

Is there something more to life
Than to build it for my wife
And to give our children more
Than their parents had before?

I go to work, earn the bread
Watch TV and go to bed
Sunrise, sunset year to year
Before I know it winter's here

But it's no scrimmage or practice game
And there's no martyr's hall of fame
Time, the speedster, takes its toll
And every day's my Superbowl

Losers live in classic style
In the never-world of "Someday I'll"
They blame bad luck each time they lose
And hide with excuses, drugs, and booze

But losing's a habit and so is winning
The way to change is by beginning
To live each day as if my last
Not in the future, nor in the past

To want it now, to dream it now
To plan it now, to do it now
To close my eyes and clearly see
That person I'd most like to be

Crystal ball, oh crystal ball
Help me hear my inner call
I think I can, I know I can
Become my greatest coach and fan
And love myself and give away
All the love I can today
I think I can, I know I can
Become a most, Uncommon Man.

Love the Children

Reach out to the children on this earth
Let them know you love them every day;
It makes no difference what their place of birth
It makes no difference how they choose to pray.

Our children are the products of
our prejudice and fear
They watch the way we live and
they remember what they see;
If we preach about our problems
and the bad things that we hear
They'll grow up exactly how
we'd hoped they'd never be.

Love the children, you were children, they're
becoming what their parents say and do. Love
the children, all the children; give them hope
that they can make their dreams come true

Reach out to the children everywhere
Regardless of their color or their creeds;
Let them know the values we all share
Show them by your actions and your deeds.

Our children are the future,
every one who's rich or poor
Let's treat them all like neighbors
even those in other lands;
And they'll learn from us to live
in peace and never think of war
Let's rejoice in being different and
reach out with helping hands

Love the children, you were children, they're
becoming what their parents say and do. Love
the children, all the children, give them hope
that they can make their dreams come true

Reach out to the children, let them know
That each has every right to happiness;
Give them hope and strength so they can grow
And learn to feel they're worthy of success

Let's keep them well and safe
and eliminate their sorrow
For as parents and their leaders
we can shape their destiny;
When we give them skills and knowledge
to create a bright tomorrow
We'll be looking in the mirror
and be proud of who we see

Love the children, you were children, they're
becoming what their parents say and do. Love
the children, all the children, give them hope
that they can make their dreams come true.

Epilogue

Seeds of Greatness

Life is a magnificent fertile garden plot given you to till, to plant, to nurture, and to reap from. What you grow in your garden is your choice. How you respond to the process along the way also is your choice.

Your garden will never be in a state of perfection. It will always be in transition.

With the end of each season is the anticipation of the next. No one season is the best, not even harvest. It has its special joys and frequent challenges, just as each of the other seasons.

To everything there is a season and place under heaven. There is a magnificent rhythm and cycle to life.

Seed to sprout. Sprout to bloom. Bloom to blossom. Blossom to Fruit.

Fruit to seed.

Success is a process. It cycles again and again. How you use the cycles to produce what benefits your life and the lives of others is up to you.

The Seeds of Greatness are the responses or attitudes you develop as a result of "seeing" the world more clearly. When you see more clearly, you see yourself as valuable and your self-esteem grows strong. Seeing clearly enables your imagination to create and soar. Seeing more clearly gives you the understanding that you are responsible for learning as much and contributing as much as you can to life.

When you see life from within, you see faith, purpose, and integrity as cornerstones of your family's foundation. You see through the eyes of love and reach out to touch and empower all those with whom you come in contact. Seeing from within is having the courage to adapt to change and to persevere when the odds seem overwhelming. Seeing from within is believing that beauty and goodness are worth planting every day.

My grandmother had planted the seeds in me as we worked in her garden, by teaching me how to "see" life. Many people go through their lives stepping on the flowers, while pointing out the weeds. Grandma taught me how to pull out the weeds, while reveling in and savoring the splendor and the fragrance of the flowers.

Whenever I find myself in a garden, my memory is flooded with images of that most special person in my life as we used to sit and talk in the shade of her plumcot tree those many years ago. I can hear her gentle words:

> *"You always get out what you put in, my child. Plant apple seeds and you get apple trees; plant the seeds of great ideas, and you will get great individuals. Do you understand what I mean?"*

I understand now. I know you understand too. ❧

About

DENIS WAITLEY

Best-selling author and speaker, Denis Waitley has painted word pictures of optimism, core values, motivation and resiliency that have become indelible and legendary in their positive impact on society. He has studied and counseled leaders in every field, including Apollo astronauts, heads of state, Fortune 500 top executives, Olympic gold medalists, and students of all ages and cultures.

THANK YOU FOR READING THIS BOOK!

If you found any of the information helpful, please take a few minutes and leave a review on the bookselling platform of your choice.

BONUS GIFT!

Don't forget to sign up to try our newsletter and grab your free personal development ebook here:

soundwisdom.com/classics

Because Your Success Matters